THE OBSERVER'S
POCKET SERIES

THE OBSERVER'S BOOK
OF FLAGS

The Observer's Books

THE OBSERVER'S BOOK OF

FLAGS·

by
I. O. EVANS, F.R.G.S.

Fully illustrated
with 83 plates in colour
and 70 line drawings

FREDERICK WARNE & CO. LTD.
FREDERICK WARNE & CO. INC.
LONDON · NEW YORK

Library of Congress Catalog
Card No. 59-8056

Printed in Great Britain

PREFACE

The aim of this book is not only to help the observer
to recognise the most important of the world's
flags but to increase his knowledge of flag-lore.
These emblems, which we all know so well, form
part of Heraldry, " the shorthand of history ": they
are at once practical, as signs of national identity,
and charged with emotional significance, as symbols
of national loyalty. Their origin and evolution is
full of interest, not always so fully realised as it
might be.

In compiling this record, I have been greatly
indebted to Mr. H. Gresham Carr, F.R.G.S., editor
of that exhaustive and authoritative volume, *Flags
of the World*, and a foremost authority on flags and
flag-lore, for placing at my disposal his voluminous
records and his expert knowledge and experience.

My thanks are also due to the College of Arms,
and especially to Mr. W. Verco, M.V.O., Rouge
Croix Pursuivant, and to the Office of the Lord Lyon
in Edinburgh, for information regarding the Royal
Emblems of England and Scotland; and to the
representatives of other Government Departments
for information regarding their respective flags.
I moreover owe much to Mr. A. F. Stuart for his
co-operation in preparing the illustrations.

Finally, I should like to place on record my debt
to the late Admiral Gordon Campbell, V.C., in
leading me to make a serious study of this fascinating
subject.

It is hoped that this brief account of the origin
and development of the world's flags may enable the
observer to realise the lofty traditions for which

these emblems stand. As Sir Edward Hamley puts it in his well-known lines, it is not so much the flag itself that stirs our souls as the deeds that were done beneath it.

This is equally true whether the deeds are those of war or of peace or of a nation " rightfully struggling to be free ": a last stand round the Regimental Colours on the battlefield, a ship going down with her one remaining gun firing and her tattered ensign waving defiantly in the breeze, a cherished emblem kept hidden until the conquerors were gone and then triumphantly rehoisted, stretcher-bearers tending the wounded under the protection of the Red Cross, a group of explorers struggling through the polar wastes with a pennant fluttering on their sledge, or two mountaineers standing on the summit of Mount Everest with the flag of the United Nations among the national emblems tied to their ice-axe.

I.O.E.

CONTENTS

INTRODUCTION

" A moth-eaten rag on a worm-eaten pole—
　It does not seem likely to stir a man's soul.
　'Tis the deeds that were done 'neath that
　　　moth-eaten rag
　When the pole was a staff and the rag was a flag."

Yet if Sir Edward Hamley, when extolling *The Old Colours of the Forty-third,* had enquired why such emblems had evoked such deeds, he would have found the enquiry would take him far back through history.

So ancient are flags that their origin is unknown. Even that of the very word " flag " is uncertain, for similar terms occur in several of the languages of north-western Europe. It may be related to " flap ", derived perhaps from the sound of a flag fluttering in the breeze.

Whatever their origin, flags are alluded to in many ancient writings. Yet they are never regarded as an innovation; their use is always taken for granted. Flags were as traditional then as they are now.

Though in very early times animal figures were used as emblems, the flags are a product of civilisation, demanding skill in weaving and dyeing. Originally perhaps mere decorative streamers or swathings on images or other ceremonial objects and later made larger and dyed or painted in

9

significant patterns, they became symbolic in themselves.

Flags are in many ways superior to other emblems. They are cheap and easy to make. Folded or rolled up, they are easy to carry or hide, and they can be unfurled at a moment's notice with dramatic suddenness. Their motion as they flutter in the breeze attracts attention and gives them a semblance of life: the Vikings, who regarded the movements of the Raven on their flags as presaging victory in battle, may not have been the only people to use such emblems as omens. Meantime, flags were useful to archers or seamen, much as the modern wind-sock is useful to airmen, in enabling them to gauge the direction and strength of the wind.

As the symbol of a king, a noble leader, or a community, flags came to be treated with respect, indeed almost with reverence. Men would gladly die to protect or capture or regain them, and on the field of battle the fight raged most fiercely around them. To capture a flag might dishearten its followers completely: the turning-point of the battle of Hastings may have been not so much the death of Harold as the fall of the Dragon Banner.

In days more pious than our own flags bore religious emblems which nobody felt it incongruous to take into battle. Several indeed are reputedly inspired by visions beheld before a victory.

HERALDRY

During the Middle Ages the design and usage of flags was codified as a branch of *Heraldry*—or, more properly, *Armory*. Flags were then emblems not of nations but of the nobility, and resembled the devices on their owners' Shields of Arms, their size giving an indication of rank.

Heraldry has produced its own technical language, using a number of terms derived from the French, with a few of Arabic origin. It also gives a specialised meaning to certain English words: the *field* of a flag, for example, signifying the background on which its emblems are placed, and the word *colour* having a restricted sense.

The hues employed in an heraldic device are called *tinctures*. They include two heraldic *metals*, *or* and *argent* (gold and silver); several *furs* or conventional mottled patterns of which one, white with black mottlings, is called *ermine* ; and *colours*. British heraldry recognises five colours only: *gules* (red, perhaps from the Arabic word for " rose "), *azure* (from the Arabic name of an ornamental stone), *vert* (green, from the French), *sable* (black), and *purpure* (purple); Continental heraldry also recognises *tenné* (orange or " tawny "). An emblem depicted in its natural colours is said to be *proper*.

It is a strict rule of heraldry that colours and metals must alternate: colour must not touch colour; nor metal, metal. If necessary they must be separated by a *fimbriation* (from the Latin *fimbria*, a fringe) a narrow border of metal or colour, as in the British Union Flag (Pl. III, 1).

Two symbols may be combined to record a marriage. They may be *dimidiated* (halved), as are the lions and ships of the Cinque Ports Flag (Pl. X, 1). The result may however seem clumsy or even grotesque, like the lions-cum-herrings in the arms of a British seaport. Or two shields-of-arms or flags may be *impaled*, placed bodily side by side

11

on one shield or flag, the husband's being on the dexter side, nearer the flagstaff (as in Pl. II, 1).

Heirs *quarter* the parental arms, dividing a shield or flag into four segments, and duplicating the arms in the upper segment on one side and the lower segment on the other; and there may be further subdivisions or variations. This method is exemplified in the British Royal Standard (Pl. I, 1) and the State Flag of Maryland (Pl. XXIX, 6).

Another method of combining emblems, freely used on flags, is to place one in the canton (see page 13) of the other. This may be used to bestow honour, as in the flag of Malta, G.C. (Pl. XXII, 2). Usually, however, it simply distinguishes one flag from another.

Needless to say, the rule forbidding two metals or colours to touch does not apply to such combined emblems: there is nothing unheraldic about the designs of the Royal Standard, the British Ensigns, or the Stars and Stripes.

MODERN FLAGS

Most of the flags of today are the emblems not of individuals but of nations and other organisations. But though they differ from the older flags in name, material, shape, design and purpose, they none the less continue the heraldic tradition.

The ceremonial colours of the armed forces are made of embroidered silk. Small cheap flags are printed on cotton. The flags intended for practical use have to be far stronger. Though experiments are being made with nylon and plastics, most are made of *bunting*, a strong woollen cloth woven in Yorkshire. The patterns are produced by sewing together cloth of different colours; small details may be added by hand. As the cloth was formerly made in pieces nine inches wide, British flags are said to be of so many nine-inch breadths: a flag a yard wide is said to of " four breadths".

Service flags may be sewn to short lengths of rope, attached to the halyards by a " toggle " passing through a rope loop. In the Royal Navy, however, they are attached to the *Inglefield clips*, ingenious metal fasteners which can be snapped together or separated at once but which cannot part accidentally. As one clip is immediately above the flag and the other at the end of a few inches of rope, there is little risk of the flag's being accidentally hoisted upside down.

A flag's *hoist* is the part nearest the flagstaff or halyard, its *fly* the part furthest away. The flag may be thought of as containing four *cantons*, the first and third in the hoist, the second and fourth in the fly. The first canton, the uppermost in the hoist, is *the* canton, and may bear a special emblem. A distinguishing *badge* may be placed in the fly.

In a restricted sense a *flag* is a square or rectangular emblem other than a personal *standard*. A *pendant* or *pennant* tapers gently towards the fly, a *triangular flag* tapers very sharply. A *burgee* normally ends in a " swallow-tail " (the term, originally *budgee*, comes from the once-famous seaport of Bugia, now Bougie, in Algeria.) These terms, however, are not strictly adhered to.

National flags are flown by governments and perhaps also by private citizens. *Merchant flags* are worn not only by commercial vessels but by passenger steamers, pleasure yachts and other unofficial craft; they may be similar to the national flags, or be simpler in design, or bear special emblems.

A national or merchant flag is worn at a vessel's stern, either at the peak or on the *ensign staff;* hence it may also form an *ensign* (from the Latin *insignia*). A flag worn at the jack-staff at a vessel's bows is the *jack*, a term of uncertain origin. The ensign or jack may or may not be similar to the national or merchant flag: a special jack or ensign may distinguish government from merchant ships. A merchant ship may fly at the mainmast head the *house flag* of its owners; when in a foreign port it may hoist at the fore a *courtesy flag*, the emblem of its temporary hosts. Flags may also be flown at the yardarm.

On appropriate occasions ships may be ceremonially *dressed*, with masthead flags as well as ensigns and jacks. When dressed " over all " they fly decorative lines of signalling flags from bow and stern to the mastheads and also either " rainbow fashion " between the mastheads, or from the mastheads to the deck.

As so many British ensigns bear the Union Flag in the canton, the term " ensign " is loosely applied to other flags of similar pattern with special cantonal emblems. Similarly the Royal Navy's use of the British Union Flag as a jack may account for its being habitually referred to as the " Union Jack ".

Among flag colours, by far the most predominant is red ; it is almost always intensely bright. Blue, the next most usual, may range from the very dark

" navy blue " to the light " air force blue ". Black is used more often than green, which colour is usually chosen because of its religious or historical associations, as by the Moslem countries and by Eire. Orange is seldom used, except when it has historical associations ; until recently it was not a fast colour. Purple is uncommon, and there are one or two other unusual hues. One fur, ermine, appears on certain personal standards. White is more frequently used than orange, and is hardly ever called " silver," whereas yellow is almost habitually spoken of as " gold ".

THE SHORTHAND OF HISTORY

Heraldry is proverbially " the shorthand of history", and many flags illustrate their historical development. The British Union Flag, and the Stars and Stripes, each commemorate the growth of a nation. Thanks partly to the French Revolution, a tricolour flag usually shows that a country gained its freedom only after an armed revolt. Since the Russian Revolution, a gold or red star has been a sign of communist ideology.

The crescent moon is a Moslem symbol. The " sun of May " on certain South American flags, like the Cap of Liberty also favoured in Latin America, is another emblem of successful revolt (though the sun and moon on the double flag of Nepal are probably of astrological significance).

The cross and the white star are emblems of democracy and the love of freedom. The cross is the symbol of Britain and the Scandinavian countries, of Switzerland and Greece. The white star has spread from the United States to Liberia and Panama ; and it was adopted quite independently in Australia and New Zealand.

The animal most depicted on flags is the lion ; the widespread use of the eagle derives from the classical tradition. Most of the other creatures displayed on flags are mythological.

A revolution involving a complete break with the national tradition is apt to evoke a flag quite different from its predecessors. One which begins as an attempt to secure a reform without a secession, or a secession without a break from national tradition, but which afterwards becomes more far-reaching, may demand first a variant of an older flag and then a completely different emblem, as is shown by the historic flags of the United States (Pl. XXIII).

A flag of ensign type, with a distinctive emblem in its canton, usually indicates British influence, either directly as in some Commonwealth countries or indirectly through the United States as in Liberia and possibly in Burma and Nationalist China.

To trace the origin and development of all flag-emblems might well throw light on the general course of human history and human thought, and on the spread of civilisation and culture. It would however demand far-reaching researches comparable to those of Sir J. G. Frazer in compiling *The Golden Bough*.

FLAG ETIQUETTE

An international etiquette of flag usage is essential, not only practically but because flags can suddenly arouse intense emotion. Grave trouble, ranging from a street brawl to a diplomatic incident, can ensue if a flag be insulted or, sometimes, even if it be ignored. To humiliate a country defeated in war its flag may be banned and replaced by some arbitrary meaningless token; to restore it to the comity of nations the use of its historic flag is resumed. As a formal ratification of the healing of a breach of diplomatic relations two nations may exchange ceremonial salutes of one another's flags.

Flags are hoisted with due ceremony at a convenient hour in the morning and normally lowered, also ceremonially, about sunset; only for special reasons are they kept flying during the night. They may be hoisted unfurled to rise fluttering to the masthead, or folded and rolled with the halyards so dexterously hitched round them that when they reach the masthead a sharp tug will break them with spectacular effect.

To fly a flag at *half mast* is the recognised token of mourning. The flag does not reach that position directly but is first raised right up and then at once lowered sufficiently to make its meaning clear.

To avoid the implication that one country is inferior to another, national flags are never, in peace-time, flown one above another. Care is taken to fly them side by side at the same height, and where possible to use flags of the same size. Most countries, however, give their own flag a slight formal precedence over those of foreigners.

To *dip* the flag is to give a ceremonial salute. At sea, the ensign is dipped; it is slightly lowered, then—lest it be mistaken for a sign of mourning— it is at once rehoisted. The salute is similarly returned, as one ship passes another. On land, the colours of the armed forces and other uniformed bodies are dipped only to Royalty or other important personages. In British usage they are lowered to touch the ground, in that of the United States they are never permitted to do so.

Other traditional ceremonies are associated with the colours. They are consecrated before being formally presented to a regiment ; they are " trooped " according to a dignified and impressive ritual ; and when taken out of service they are hung on the walls of a parish church or cathedral.

Among civilians there is much diversity of usage. The *flag code* of the United States has also been adopted in other lands. In Britain there is no formal code, the individual being largely free to use his own judgment. In every land common sense and courtesy, the instinctive desire to show respect to an emblem so fraught with meaning, should be a sufficient guide.

GREAT BRITAIN

THE ROYAL STANDARD

As the personal emblem of the Sovereign of Great Britain and the Commonwealth, the *Royal Standard* (Pl. I, 1) denotes the presence of H.M. the Queen. Except that when flown over Westminster Abbey it may mean either that she is in the Abbey itself or in its vicinity, when flown over a building it signifies that she has entered it ; when hoisted at a vessel's masthead, that she is on board.

Its first and fourth quarters bear the Royal Emblem of England, its second that of Scotland, its third that of Ireland. The three lions (heraldic leopards) of England appeared on a great seal of Richard I. The rampant lion within its tressure is not a national flag but a royal symbol of Scotland ; it was used about 1165 by William the Lion. The Irish Harp was displayed at the funeral of Queen Elizabeth I.

This quartering is the result of historical development. From Edward III to Elizabeth I the English sovereigns showed their claim to the French throne by quartering the lilies, gold on blue, of France with the English lions, and giving the lilies precedence. James I placed this flag in its entirety in the first and fourth quarters of his Standard, with the rampant lion in the second and the harp in the third. William III placed at its centre a small shield displaying the Lion of Nassau, and impaled this Standard with that of his wife Mary, which was similar to that of James.

To signalise the Union of England and Scotland, Queen Anne placed in the first and fourth quarters of her standard the three lions impaled with the rampant lion, leaving the harp in the third but relegating the lilies of France to the second. George I substituted in the fourth quarter the threefold Arms of Hanover. In 1802, after the Treaty of Amiens, George III dropped the lilies completely, restored the rampant lion to the second quarter, and placed the lions of England in both the first and the fourth ; a shield, ensigned with a crown, at the flag's centre, bore the Hanoverian Arms. These were removed completely at the accession of Queen Victoria, and, minor changes apart, the Royal Standard took its present form.

As a Principality *Wales* has its own Standard. This displays arms borne in the thirteenth century by Owen Glendower : two red lions on gold quartered with two gold on red.

In 1960 it was announced that the Queen had decided to adopt a new Personal Standard of

distinctive design for use on special occasions. It was not intended to supplant the Royal Standard. It consists of the initial E ensigned with the Royal Crown, the whole within a chaplet of roses, all in gold, on a blue field, having a gold fringe on three sides.

PERSONAL STANDARDS OF THE ROYAL FAMILY

The Personal Standard of the Prince Philip, Duke of Edinburgh (Pl. I, 2) is quartered and displays three blue lions with nine red hearts on gold (Denmark) ; a white cross on blue (Greece) ; two vertical stripes, black on white (Mountbatten) ; and a black castle with three red domes on white (Edinburgh).

The Standard of Queen Elizabeth the Queen Mother (Pl. II, 1) impales the Royal Standard with her own family arms, those of Bowes-Lyon. These quarter the rampant lion and tressure, blue on white, with three long-bows proper on ermine— a striking example of punning heraldry!

Children of the Sovereign place near the upper edge of the Standard a white " label with three points ". That of the Princess Margaret (1) bears the Scottish thistle on its centre point and the Tudor rose on the outer points. That of the Duke of Gloucester has a St. George's Cross on the outer points and a red lion on the centre point (2), that of the Princess Royal a St. George's Cross on

1. The Royal Standard

2. The Duke of Edinburgh

PLATE I. GREAT BRITAIN

all three (3). The label of the Duke of Kent, a grandson of King George V, has five points, on which a blue anchor alternates with the St. George's Cross (4). The Standard of the Prince of Wales (Pl. II, 2) comprises the Royal Standard bearing a shield of the Arms of Wales, ensigned with his Coronet, in the centre thereof.

The label of the Duke of Windsor, in token of his former rank as King Edward VIII, bears a Royal Crown on its centre point; so far it has appeared

1. The Queen Mother

2. The Prince of Wales

PLATE II. GREAT BRITAIN. PERSONAL STANDARDS

only on his Arms. Other members of the Royal
Family—the Duchess of Gloucester and the Duchess
of Kent—fly a Royal Standard with an ermine
border.

THE UNION FLAG

Like the Royal Standard, the British Union Flag is
a composite emblem. Though it is not clear how
the Cross of St. George became the symbol of
England, its use has long been traditional. It

forms the National Flag of England, a red cross on a white field (Pl. III, 3).

According to tradition, St. Andrew, when condemned to death, feeling himself unworthy to suffer exactly as had his Lord, was crucified on two diagonal beams ; his relics, after a shipwreck, were cast up on the coast of Scotland, where they were long treasured ; and a diagonal cross was seen in the sky by the Scottish King Achaius, who adopted it as his national emblem. It has for centuries formed the National Flag of Scotland : a white saltire (diagonal cross) on a blue field (Pl. IV, 1).

Anxious to symbolise his rule of both countries on a new flag, James I instructed his heralds to design a composite emblem. This was difficult, for two symbols cannot possibly occupy places of equal honour on the same flag ; the emblem chosen evoked a storm of unavailing protest, that of the Scots being especially vehement. The St. George's Cross, duly fimbriated in white, with the St. Andrew's Saltire as its field, gave "Greater Britain" its first Union Flag in 1606 (Pl. III, 2).

James commanded his sea-faring subjects to fly this Union flag at the main-top, and to fly in the fore-top either the Red Cross of " South Britain " or the White Cross of "North Britain". Charles I, however, reserved the Union exclusively for Royal vessels, merchantmen using only one of the older crosses. It fell into disuse during the Commonwealth, but at the Restoration it once more became exclusively a Royal emblem, though British merchantmen might now fly instead of one of the older flags, a red flag with a small canton bearing the St. George's Cross. Under Queen Anne the Mer-

24

chant Flag became a Red Ensign with the James Union in the canton, the Union itself remaining an emblem of the Royal service.

Though St. Patrick devoted himself to missionary work among the Irish, who still cherish his memory, the so-called " St. Patrick's Cross " has no associations with him and but tenuous ones with the Irish : it is the heraldic device, centuries old, of a noble family which though long resident in Ireland is of Welsh origin. Possibly, on the union of Great Britain with Ireland in 1801, it was selected as being the only emblem with Irish associations to harmonise with the James Union. It is a red saltire on a white field (Pl. III, 4).

It had, however, to be modified. To give the Scottish emblem the place of greater honour (at the top of the hoist) to which it was entitled as the earlier on the flag, the two saltires were counterchanged, white above red in the hoist and red above white in the fly (Pl. III, 5). The red saltire was also given the usual fimbriation.

Such was the development of a flag whose design is at once original, harmonious and striking. The Union Flag thus formed is the emblem not only of Great Britain and Northern Ireland but of the British Commonwealth of Nations (Pl. III, 1).

This development has made it unsymmetrical, its hoist differing from its fly in the arrangement of the two saltires. In the hoist the broad white stripe is above the red, and it is thus that the flag is correctly—and should always be—flown.

The Union Flag is popularly, though quite inaccurately, called the " Union Jack "—a term properly used only when a vessel of the Royal Navy

25

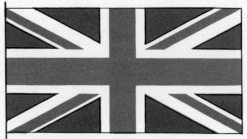

1. Union Flag

2. First Union Flag (1606)

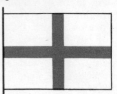

3. Cross of St. George

4. Cross of St. Patrick

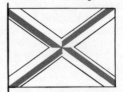

Counterchange of saltires

PLATE III. GREAT BRITAIN

PLATE IV. (Opposite)
GREAT BRITAIN. REGIONAL EMBLEMS

1. Scotland. Cross of St. Andrew

2. Wales

3. Northern Ireland

4. Jersey

5. Isle of Man

6. Guernsey

wears it at the jack-staff. The origin of this term is uncertain. It may come from the " jack ", (an archaic term for a soldier's sleeveless tunic) which at one time displayed a national emblem, or from the Latin or French forms of James : Jacobus or Jacques ; or, more probably, it derives from the custom, dating from Stuart days, that Royal vessels should wear a small Union Flag on the bowsprit, " jack " being a naval colloquialism for " small ". Incorrect as it is, the usage is so widely spread that it is never likely to be eradicated.

REGIONAL EMBLEMS

Every region of Britain has its own emblem, but that of *England*, the St. George's Cross (Pl. III, 3) is far less frequently used than that of *Scotland*, the St. Andrew's Saltire (Pl. IV, 1). The rampant lion and tressure, as in the second quarter of the Royal Standard, although it is really a Royal symbol, is also much used, though quite unofficially, as a Scottish national flag.

The traditional emblem of *Wales* is the red dragon on a white and green field (Pl. IV, 2).

The St. George's Cross with the ancient regional emblem, the blood-red Right Hand of Ulster, at its centre surmounted by the Royal Crown, forms the flag of Northern Ireland (Pl. IV, 3). A shield bearing the similar emblem and surrounded by a wreath at the centre of the Union forms the flag of the Governor of Northern Ireland.

The symbol of the *Isle of Man* is the Trinacria, three armoured legs, in white and yellow, meeting at the thigh. Reputed to be of Sicilian origin, it may have been introduced into Britain in the thirteenth century by Alexander III of Scotland. Surrounded by a garland at the centre of the Union it is the distinguishing flag of the Lieutenant-Governor; placed on a red field it forms the island's National Flag. (Pl. IV, 5).

In the Channel Islands, *Jersey* and *Guernsey* still use the ancient emblem of England, the three Lions, in gold, on a red shield, that of Guernsey being differenced by a sprig of golden leaves at the top of the shield (Pl. IV, 4, 6); at the centre of the Union these form the flags of the respective Lieutenant-Governors. The National Flags of *Jersey* and *Guernsey* consist respectively of the emblems of St. Patrick and St. George (Pl. III, 4, 3); but the latter may be flown only on land.

 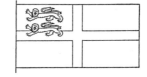

The flag of *Alderney* is a St. George's Cross with a green gold-bordered circle at its centre displaying a gold lion holding a sprig of leaves. The Seigneural Flag of *Sark* is also a St. George's Cross, with two gold lions in the canton, the lower of the two impinging on the arm of the Cross.

THE QUEEN'S REPRESENTATIVES

In Scotland certain officials, as representing the Sovereign, may in appropriate circumstances fly

1. Governor-General of Canada

2. Ambassador

3. Consular Officer (ashore)

PLATE V. THE QUEEN'S REPRESENTATIVES

the Standard of the King of the Scots as in the second quarter of the Royal Standard (Pl. I, 1).

The Governors-General of the Dominions and certain other regions of the Commonwealth fly dark blue flags displaying the Royal Crest, the lion surmounting the Crown, with a scroll bearing the region's name (Pl. V, 1). Other regional Governors or Lieutenant-Governors place the appropriate badge on a white disc within a garland of laurel at the centre of the Union Flag, as for example in Northern Ireland and the Isle of Man.

Ambassadors and Ministers similarly place within

1. White Ensign

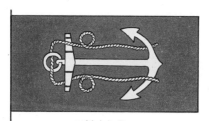

2. Admiralty Flag

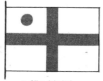

3. Vice Admiral

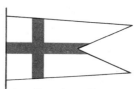

4. Commodore 1st Class

PLATE VI. THE ROYAL NAVY

31

the garland the Royal Arms (Pl. V, 2). Consular Officers when on shore display at the centre of the Union a Royal Crown on a white disc without a garland (Pl. V, 3) ; when afloat they fly as a Jack a Blue Ensign with the Royal Arms in its fly.

A Lord Lieutenant of a County flies a Union Flag which displays at its centre a Royal Crown above a sword placed horizontally with its point towards the fly. A Queen's Harbour Master has a special flag, the Union surrounded with a broad white border ; a white circle at its centre bears the Royal Crown above the letters " Q. H. M.".

THE ROYAL NAVY

The distinguishing flag of the Royal Navy—it is also used by the Royal Yacht Squadron—is the *White Ensign*, a St. George's Cross with the Union Flag in the canton (Pl. VI, 1). A similar flag, with an heraldic garter at its centre surrounding the Royal Cypher and ensigned with the Crown, gives the Royal Navy its *Queen's Colour*.

Two other emblems exclusive to the Royal Navy are the *Masthead Pendant*, a long tapering flag with the St. George's Cross in the hoist, worn to show that a vessel is in commission, and the *Union Jack* correctly so styled, a Union Flag at the jackstaff ; this is not normally worn when a vessel is under way.

The supreme command of the Navy is symbolised by the *Admiralty Flag*, which displays an anchor, gold on a red field (Pl. VI, 2). It flies, by day and night, over the Admiralty buildings in London, and is hoisted in any vessel on which two or more of the Lords of the Admiralty are embarked, or in any Navy vessel during her launching. It is also flown in any vessel on which H.M. the Queen embarks, for she is the source from which the Admiralty derives its powers. It is never dipped in salute, and is half-masted only on the death of the Sovereign.

The *Command Flags* of the Royal Navy, the emblems of the flag officers, are, for an Admiral of the Fleet a Union Flag, for an Admiral the St. George's Cross, and for a Commodore 1st Class, the Broad Pendant (Pl. VI, 4), a similar flag but tapering slightly and with a " swallow-tail ". The flags of a Vice-Admiral (Pl. VI, 3) and a Commodore 2nd Class place in the canton of the respective flags a red ball ; that of a Rear Admiral adds a second red ball in the third quarter.

Undefaced, the *Blue Ensign*—similar to the Red Ensign (Pl. IX, 1) but with its field blue instead of red—is the emblem of the Royal Naval Reserve.

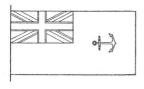

With a distinguishing badge in its fly, it is used by several organisations. The badge of Royal Fleet Auxiliary vessels is a golden anchor, placed horizontally. That of the Royal Naval Minewatching Service depicts a floating

C

33

mine encircled by a length of cable ensigned by a naval crown. That of the Sea Cadet Corps shows a foul anchor within a circle bearing the name of the Corps ; above is a naval crown and below is the Corps motto " Ready Aye Ready."

THE ROYAL MARINES

The design on the Colours of the Royal Marines includes a foul anchor, a terrestrial globe within a laurel wreath, the name " Gibraltar " and the motto *Per mare per terram* (By sea, by land). On the Union Flag it forms the Queen's Colour, on the Blue Ensign the Regimental Colour.

THE BRITISH ARMY

Not until 1938 did the British Army have its own flag, and then King George V approved an Army Badge and Flag. This consists of the Royal Crest superimposed upon two crossed swords ; in the *Army Flag* it appears on a red field (Pl. VII, 1).

With certain exceptions, the combatant units of the Army have their own individual Colours, derived from the banners of the noblemen who formerly led them. A Cavalry Regiment carries one Colour only, either a rectangular Standard or a Guidon (originally *guide-homme*, a guide to the men) which has its fly slit and the two halves rounded ; but Light Cavalry Regiments use instead of Colours their richly-embroidered Drum Banners.

34

1. Army Flag

2. G.O.C. (afloat)

3. Army Council

PLATE VII. THE BRITISH ARMY

Infantry Units, other than Rifle Regiments, carry two Colours. In the Foot Guards the Queen's Colour is crimson, though perhaps with a small Union Flag in the canton, the Regimental Colour is the Union Flag. In the Line Regiments it is the Union Flag which forms the Queen's Colour; the Regimental Colour has a field the hue of the Regiment's facings, but if these be white it bears a cross of St. George type but with unusually broad arms. The Colours bear the Regimental Badge, and also the Unit's " Battle Honours," the names of famous engagements in which it distinguished itself.

The emblem of the Army Council is a shield bearing the Arms of the Board of Ordnance, three antique field-pieces and three cannon-balls (Pl. VII, 3). That of the General Officer Commanding, when afloat, consists of the Royal Cypher and Crown on a blue circle surrounded by a laurel-wreath (Pl. VII, 2). These emblems appear at the centre of the Union Flag.

Other Army badges appear in the fly of the Blue Ensign. The shield of the Ordnance and Royal Artillery is somewhat similar to that of the Army Council. The badge of the Royal Army Service Corps consists of the traditional crossed swords.

The emblem of the Royal Engineers depicts a winged hand arising from a mural crown and releasing flashes of lightning.

THE ROYAL AIR FORCE

Though now independent, the Royal Air Force originated from branches of the older Services; its emblems therefore combine with its own " Air Force blue " the dark Navy blue and the Army's red. Its flag is the sky-blue *R.A.F. Ensign*, with the Union in the canton and the familiar roundel (" target ") in the fly : a red disc within concentric circles of white and dark blue (Pl. VIII, 1).

The Queen's Colour of the R.A.F. resembles the Ensign but bears the Royal Cypher and Crown at its centre. The Queen's Colour for individual

Units and the Standard for operational squadrons bear appropriate emblems on a field of R.A.F. blue. The Command Flags are light blue variously striped dark blue and red.

Two R.A.F. Ensigns bear distinguishing badges instead of the Roundel. The badge of the Royal Observer Corps shows, encircled by a laurel wreath surmounted by the Royal Crown, the figure of an Elizabethan Coast Watcher holding aloft a blazing

torch, with the motto " Forewarned is Forearmed". That of the Air Training Corps displays a falcon ; above is an astral crown and below is the Corps motto " Venture Adventure". The British Ocean Weather Ships, though part of the Air Ministry's meteorological service, wear not the light blue but the dark blue Ensign ; their badge depicts the sun rising over the sea, with the R.A.F. Eagle, in gold and dark blue, in the foreground.

1. Royal Air Force Ensign

2. Civil Air Ensign

PLATE VIII. GREAT BRITAIN. AIR ENSIGNS

THE CIVIL AIR SERVICE

The field of the *Civil Air Ensign* is R.A.F. blue; it is charged with a dark blue cross, duly fimbriated in white, of St. George type (Pl. VIII, 2). It may be flown over British civil airfields and by the offices of British air transport undertakings, and also by British aircraft when grounded.

1. Merchant Flag

2. Commissioners of Northern Lighthouses

3. Commissioners of Irish Lights

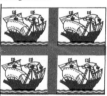

4. Trinity House Jack

5. Royal National Lifeboat Institution

PLATE IX. GREAT BRITAIN. MERCHANT NAVY, LIGHTHOUSE AND PILOTAGE AUTHORITIES

A dark blue pennant, displaying the Crown over a post-horn in yellow and bearing appropriate wording in white, is the *Royal Air Mail Flag* and is flown by aircraft carrying Mail.

THE MERCHANT SERVICE

Unless officially authorised to wear the Blue Ensign of the Royal Naval Reserve, ships of the British Merchant Service wear the well-known *Red Ensign*, sometimes facetiously referred to as the " Red Duster". In the canton is the Union Flag, and its field is ideally a vivid red. It is worn not only by merchant ships but by passenger vessels, pleasure yachts, and fishing-craft (Pl. IX, 1).

Some merchant ships wear at the jackstaff a white-bordered Union Flag, the so-called " Pilot Merchant Jack ". A small white pennant flown at the fore yard-arm and displaying a post-horn below the Crown is the *Royal Mail Flag*.

THE LIGHTHOUSE AND LIFE-BOAT SERVICES

Trinity House is responsible for the lighthouses of England and Wales and for pilotage throughout the British Isles. Its emblem consists of a St. George's Cross quartering four sailing ships of the Tudor period, black on a blue heraldic sea ; with distinguishing emblems at its centre it forms the Master's and the Deputy Master's Flags ; it appears in the fly of the Trinity House Red Ensign and on the red Trinity House Burgee (or cornet), and itself forms the Trinity House Jack (Pl. IX, 4).

The flag of the Commissioners of Northern Lighthouses, which form the General Lighthouse Authority for Scotland and the Isle of Man, is unique in that it consists of a white ensign *without* the usual St. George's Cross, and its canton consists of the First Union Flag—that authorised when the Authority was constituted in 1786 ; in the fly is depicted a lighthouse (Pl. IX, 2).

The flag of the Commissioners of Irish Lights (Pl. IX, 3) is somewhat similar to that of Trinity House but quarters two lighthouses with two lightships.

The flag of the Royal National Life-boat Institution also bears a St. George's Cross, but this is edged with dark blue ; at its centre appears the Royal Crown above a foul anchor, and in its quarters are the letters " R.N.L.I." (Pl. IX, 5).

THE CINQUE PORTS

The Cinque Ports Flag is flown by the Lord Warden, an office held by Sir Winston Churchill. It bears three stylised representations of Dover Castle, gold on blue, in the first quarter and a larger single one in the fourth ; in the left halves of the second and third quarter respectively appear, red on gold, a peer's coronet above an anchor, and a sailing ship ; in the right halves of each are three lions dimidiated with ship's hulls (Pl. X, 1).

THE CIVIL DEFENCE SERVICE

The Ensign of the Civil Defence Service is quartered ; in the canton is the Union Flag ; the second and third quarters are yellow ; the fourth,

1. Cinque Ports

2. Corporation of Lloyds

3. London County Council

4. Civil Defence Service

PLATE X. GREAT BRITAIN. MISCELLANEOUS FLAGS AND BADGES

which is dark blue, may display the Royal Crown above the letters " C.D." (Pl. X, 4).

CIVIC FLAGS

The St. George's Cross, red on white, distinguishes a number of civic flags associated with London. That of the City of London bears in the canton, in red, the sword which beheaded St. Paul. The Cross on the badge of the London County Council is placed above the six blue and white wavy bars which represent water and below a

42

mural crown ; at its centre appears a gold lion (Pl. X, 3). The badge appears on a white field.

On the shield which forms the badge of the Corporation of Lloyd's the Cross and Sword of London City are placed above a foul anchor in gold (Pl. X, 2). Lloyd's signal stations fly a blue ensign with this badge in the fly ; Lloyd's burgee for boats places it in the canton of a long pennant whose field shows a St. George's Cross with its arms traversed by a very narrow blue cross.

At the centre of the St. George's Cross on the House Flag of the Port of London Authority is a circle with a representation of St. Paul dominating the Tower of London ; the badge on the P.L.A. Blue Ensign depicts a sea-lion grasping a trident.

THE BRITISH COMMONWEALTH

Most of the emblems of the Commonwealth indicate in varying degrees unity with Britain. In Canada, Australia, and New Zealand, most of whose inhabitants are of British descent, the canton of the regional ensign bears the British Union Flag ; this also applies to many of the Colonies. In the Republic of South Africa, a former member of the Commonwealth, the British emblem appears, though less conspicuously, on the National Flag. In the Asian Commonwealth countries no British emblem appears on the regional flags, but the flag usage of the regional navies still commemmorates their former association with the Royal Navy.

CANADA

The distinctive flag—which is also the Merchant Flag—of the Dominion of Canada is the Red Ensign charged in the fly with the Dominion's Shield of Arms. The upper part of the shield resembles the Royal Standard except that—in token of the share of the French in the nation's development—its fourth quarter displays the three *fleurs-de-lis* (lilies), gold on blue, which form the historical emblem of France ; below appears the traditional emblem of Canada itself, three green maple leaves on a white field (Pl. XI, 1).

The Blue Ensign, similarly charged, forms the

Government Flag and the Jack of the Royal
Canadian Navy. The Ensign of the Royal Canadian
Air Force resembles that of the R.A.F., but replaces
the central disc by a red maple leaf. The badge of
the Royal Canadian Air Cadets places the Maple
Leaf above an albatross in flight.

Two of the Canadian Provinces have their own
flags. The *fleurdelisé* flag of *Quebec* bears a broad
white cross of St. George type quartering four
white fleurs-de-lis on a light blue field (Pl. XI, 2).
The flag of *Nova Scotia*, based on the Coat-of-Arms
granted by Charles I, combines the two Scottish
emblems : the rampant lion and tressure at the
centre of the St. Andrew's Saltire, which however
has its colours reversed (Pl. XI, 3).

The other provinces have distinctive badges which
appear in the fly of the Ensigns. *Newfoundland*
still uses the emblem which it adopted when it
formed a separate Dominion : Mercury, the god
of travel and trade, besides whom kneels a seaman,
indicates a boat to Britannia ; the motto *Haec Tibi
Dona Fero* might be translated, " I bring you these
gifts " (Pl. XII, 10).

The badges of the rest of the provinces consist

45

1. National Flag

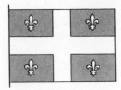

2. Quebec

3. Nova Scotia

PLATE XI. CANADA

of shields (Pl. XII), on which one of the emblems of the mother country appears above a regional symbol : the lymphad (heraldic ship) of *New Brunswick* (4) ; the oak-tree and three saplings of *Prince Edward Island* (8) with the motto *Parva sub Ingenti* (" Small beside great ") ; the three maple leaves, gold on green, of *Ontario* (5) ; the buffalo of *Manitoba* (3) ; the three wheatsheaves, gold on green, of *Saskatchewan* (6) ; the wheatfields with a prairie separating them from the Rocky Mountains, of *Alberta* (1) ; and the sun emblem, against an heraldic sea, of *British Columbia*, with the motto " *Splendor Sine Occasu* " (" Splendour that never sets ") (2).

Recently the two Canadian Territories have been

1. Alberta

2. British Columbia
SPLENDOR·SINE·OCCASU

3. Manitoba

4. New Brunswick

5. Ontario

6. Saskatchewan

7. Yukon

8. Prince Edward Island
PARVA·SUB·INGENT

9. North-West Territories

10. Newfoundland
TERRA NOVA
HÆC·TIBI·DONA·FERO

PLATE XII. BADGES OF CANADIAN PROVINCES AND TERRITORIES

granted their own emblems, each consisting of a shield with one regional symbol appearing above another. That of the *Yukon Territory* places a circle of vair, an heraldic fur, at the centre of a St. George's Cross in the upper part of its shield ; below this two red triangles with their points upward and fimbriated in white, and each charged with two gold circles represent the mountains with their mineral wealth ; the field is blue, and down its centre runs a wavy white stripe with a narrow wavy blue stripe along its centre symbolising the Yukon River flowing through the snow. (Pl. XII, 7).

In the shield of the *North-West Territories* a wavy blue line crossing a white field horizontally represents the North-West Passage through the icefields ; below this the shield is divided diagonally by a wavy line representing the " timber line " between tundra and forest ; on one section of the shield gold billets on green indicate the minerals and on the other the face of a white fox on red represents fur-trapping. (Pl. XII, 9).

AUSTRALIA

The National Flag of the Commonwealth of Australia—and the Jack of the Royal Australian Navy—is an ensign of royal blue with the Union Flag in the canton ; in the fly are depicted, in white, the five principal stars in the Southern Cross constellation, and below the canton appears a larger emblem, the " Commonwealth Star," which is purely symbolic (Pl. XIII, 1).

The Merchant Flag places the Southern Cross and the Commonwealth Star on the Red Ensign. In the Ensigns of the Royal Australian Air Force

48

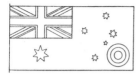

and the Australian Civil Air Service these emblems are adapted to harmonise with the designs of the corresponding British Ensigns.

The circular badges of the six Australian States, which appear in the fly of the Blue Ensign, are based on their respective coats-of-arms (Pl. XIII, 2–7). Those of the four eastern States are heraldic: that of *New South Wales* (2) consists of a St. George's Cross, with the gold Lion of England at its centre and a star on each of its arms; that of *Victoria* (7) displays the Southern Cross, as on the Australian Flag, surmounted by the Royal Crown; that of *Queensland* (3) places the Crown at the centre of a blue Maltese Cross on a white field; and that of *Tasmania* (5) is a lion, red on white. The emblems of the other two States depict, on a yellow field, birds familiar in those regions: in *South Australia* (4) a white-backed piping shrike, with its wings displayed; in *Western Australia* (6) the famous black swan.

The Territories of *Papua* and *New Guinea*, being administered by the Australian Government, use the same Ensigns—blue for the National and Government Flags and red for the Merchant Flag—as Australia itself.

NEW ZEALAND

Though the Ensigns of the Dominion of New Zealand also display the Southern Cross, they differ from those of Australia in showing only its

1. National Flag

2. New South Wales   3. Queensland   4. South Australia

5. Tasmania   6. Western Australia   7. Victoria

PLATE XIII. AUSTRALIA

four principal stars; nor do they bear anything
corresponding to the Australian Commonwealth
Star. On the Blue Ensign, which forms the
Government Flag, the stars are red fimbriated in
white; on the Red Ensign, which forms the
Merchant Flag, they are white (Pl. XIV, 1, 2).

1. N.Z. Government Flag and Jack

2. N.Z. Merchant Flag

3. Western Samoa

PLATE XIV. NEW ZEALAND AND WESTERN SAMOA

Ships of the Royal New Zealand Navy wear the White Ensign, and fly the Masthead Pendant, of the Royal Navy. However, the Blue Ensign is worn *as a Jack* for distinguishing purposes when ships are at anchor, or under way and dressed with masthead flags. The last mentioned comprise the aforesaid Blue Ensign and the White Ensign; these are hoisted at the main and fore respectively.

The Ensign of the Royal New Zealand Air Force resembles that of the Royal Air Force except that it places the letters " NZ " in white on the central disc. The New Zealand Civil Air Ensign is similar to that of Britain, but displays the Southern Cross in the fourth quarter.

WESTERN SAMOA. The flag is similar to the British Red Ensign except that its canton is blue and displays a Southern Cross of *five* stars, resembling not that of New Zealand itself but that of Australia (Pl. XIV, 3).

INDIA

The National Flag of the Republic of India—and, in smaller size, the Jack—is a horizontal tricolour of saffron, white and green; on the central stripe, in dark blue, appears the *Chakra* (wheel) of the Buddhist king Asoka, a symbol of peaceful change (Pl. XV, 1).

The President's Flag is quartered blue and red, and displays in gold outline the three Asoka Lions which form the State Emblem of India, an elephant, a pair of scales, and a lotus bowl: these respectively symbolise unity, patience and strength, justice with economy, and plenty.

The Ensign of the Indian Navy is white with a red cross of St. George type—a symbol of its association with the other navies of the Commonwealth—and the National Flag in the canton. The Merchant Flag is red with the National Flag in the canton. The National Flag similarly forms the canton of the Indian Air Force Ensign, which is light blue; the roundel in the fly consists of a green disc surrounded by concentric circles of white and saffron.

PAKISTAN

The National Flag and the Ensign of the Republic of Pakistan bears the Mohammedan emblem of the crescent moon and star on a field of bottle-green; a broad white stripe down the hoist represents the Republic's non-Moslem peoples (Pl. XV, 2). The Merchant Flag is a red ensign, with the National Flag in the first quarter. The Jack is dark green with a modified form of the crescent and star above its centre and a foul anchor in white in each of the lower corners.

The Ensign of the Pakistan Air Force places the National Flag in the canton; its field is air force blue, and the target in its fly is a white circle surrounded by a green ring.

CEYLON

The National Flag of the Dominion of Ceylon originally resembled the Sinhalese Royal Flag of the last King of Kandy; on a crimson field with a gold border and a gold pinnacle or spire in each

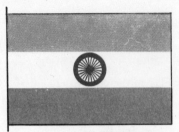

1. INDIA. National Flag and Jack

2. PAKISTAN. National Flag and Ensign

3. CEYLON. National Flag

PLATE XV. THE BRITISH COMMONWEALTH IN ASIA

1. Federation of Malaya

2. Singapore

3. British North Borneo

4. Hong Kong

5. Sarawak

6. Brunei State Flag

7. Maldives. National Flag

PLATE XVI. MALAYA AND SINGAPORE. BADGES OF BRITISH COLONIES IN THE FAR EAST. BRITISH PROTECTED STATES

corner appears, also in gold, a lion grasping a sword. To make this " Lion Flag " representative of all the country's peoples, vertical stripes of green and saffron were later added in the hoist (Pl. XV, 3).

This flag forms the canton of all the Ensigns: white with a St. George's Cross for the Royal Ceylon Navy; red for the Merchant Flag; blue for Naval Auxiliaries and, with distinguishing badges, for Government and Customs vessels.

The earlier National Flag forms the canton of the Air Force Ensign; its field is light blue and in the fly are two horizontal stripes, saffron over green, on which is a red disc with a gold centre.

MALAYA

The Flag of the Federation of Malaya (Pl. XVI, 1) combines the royal colour, gold, of the Malayan Sultans with the national colours of Britain. The canton displays the Mohammedan crescent and star in gold on a blue field; the fly consists of eleven red and white horizontal stripes, one stripe—and one point of the star in the canton—for each of the Federation's component States. These have their own State Flags, mostly very simple in design.

SINGAPORE

The flag of Singapore (Pl. XVI, 2) is divided horizontally red over white; in the upper portion there is a crescent and five stars in white, each star having five points. Red is said to represent the brotherhood and equality of man, and white symbolises purity and virtue; the crescent stands for a young country and the five stars for democracy, peace, progress, justice, and equality.

THE FAR EAST

The badge of *Sarawak* (Pl. XVI, 5), based on the flag of the former Rajah, Sir Charles Brooke, is a shield bearing on gold a cross of St. George type divided vertically black and red, with an antique crown at its centre. That of *North Borneo* (Pl. XVI, 3) comes from the crest of the Coat-of-Arms: from a gold and blue wreath rise two arms, one that of a native, the other that of a white man; the two hands grasp a yellow flag displaying a red lion.

The badge of *Hong Kong* includes a shield displaying a naval crown above two junks at sea, and supported by a lion and a Chinese dragon; the crest shows a crowned lion holding a pearl (Pl. XVI, 4).

The State Flag of *Brunei* is yellow, and is crossed diagonally by a broad stripe divided lengthwise white over black (Pl. XVI, 6). The National and Merchant Flag of the *Maldive Islands* is red with a green rectangle at its centre and a black and white stripe in the hoist; a white crescent appears on the green rectangle (Pl. XVI, 7). The Sultan's Flag bears the Mohammedan white crescent and star.

AFRICAN FEDERATIONS AND COLONIES

The shield which forms the badge of the *Federation of Rhodesia and Nyasaland* combines emblems from the badges formerly used by the three colonies from which it was formed, the " dovetailing " indicating their unification. From Nyasaland comes a gold sun rising against a blue sky; from Southern Rhodesia a lion, red on white, part of the arms of the Rhodes family; and from Northern Rhodesia thirteen black and white wavy bars suggestive of the Victoria Falls (Pl. XVII, 1).

1. Rhodesia
and
Nyasaland

2. Kenya

3. Zanzibar

4. Tanganyika

5. Uganda

PLATE XVII.

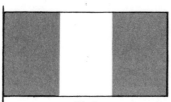

1. Nigeria

2. Ghana

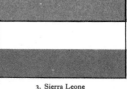

3. Sierra Leone

PLATE XVIII.

The *Federation of Nigeria's* badge was super-
seded by a flag when it became independent. It
consists of three vertical stripes of equal width,
green, white and green (Pl. XVIII, 1).

Some of the African colonies have distinctive
badges placed on the Blue Ensign. The badge of
Kenya (Pl. XVII, 2) displays a rampant lion, that of
Gambia (p. 60) an elephant beside a palm-tree.

The badge of *Basutoland* (p. 60) shows a fleece
between two wheatsheaves above a crocodile. The
ornate shield of *St. Helena* (p. 60) represents an
Indiaman sailing between two cliffs.

The Standard, Ensign and Merchant Flags of
Zanzibar are plain red, but the badge of the British

Resident, placed at the centre of the Union Flag, depicts a *dhow* at sea; above is the Royal Crown (Pl. XVII, 3).

TANGANYIKA

Tanganyika has dropped the badge and replaced it with a flag consisting of three horizontal stripes of equal width, green over black over green, the colours being separated by narrow yellow stripes (Pl. XVII, 4).

UGANDA

The old badge has given way to a new flag. It consists of six horizontal stripes of equal width: black, yellow, red, black, yellow, red; in the centre thereof a white disc bearing a Crested Crane (Pl. XVII, 5).

GHANA

The Flag of the Independent State of Ghana is a horizontal tricolour, red, gold and green. On the central stripe is a five-pointed black star (Pl. XVIII, 2). The red stripe represents those who worked to gain the country's independence, the yellow the riches of the country and its old name of the Gold Coast, the green its forests and arable land; the black star stands for African freedom.

SIERRA LEONE

Sierra Leone has replaced its badge with a new flag, comprising a horizontal tricolour, green over white over blue (Pl. XVIII, 3).

THE WEST INDIES

Several of the islands, as well as the groups of islands, have their own badges (Pls. XIX, XX), displayed on the Union Flag or on the Blue or Red Ensigns. On many of these appear stretches of coastal scenery, though others are heraldic.

Jamaica now has a distinctive flag (Pl. XX, 1), consisting of a field divided diagonally; the triangles thus formed are black at the hoist and fly and green top and bottom; overall a diagonal cross in gold.

The badge of *Grenada* shows a square-sailed vessel heading for a distant shore; the Latin motto *Clarior e Tenebris* means " Bright out of Darkness " (Pl. XIX, 3).

The new flag of *Trinidad and Tobago* (Pl. XIX, 1) consists of a red field on which a diagonal black band, bordered in white, runs downwards from left

1. Trinidad and Tobago

2. Leeward Islands

3. Grenada

CLARIOR E TENEBRIS

MISCERIQUE

FŒDERA JUNGI

PROBAT POPULOS ET

4. Trinidad
and
Tobago
(former badge)

5. Barbados

BARBADOS

6. Turks and Caicos Islands

TURKS and CAICOS
ISLANDS

PLATE XIX. THE WEST INDIES

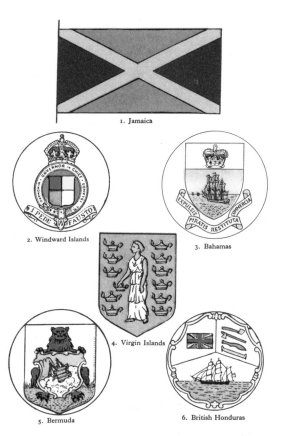

1. Jamaica

2. Windward Islands

3. Bahamas

4. Virgin Islands

5. Bermuda

6. British Honduras

PLATE XX. THE WEST INDIES

to right. The former badge represented a harbour in which were several vessels; the motto *Miscerique Probat Populos et Foedera Jungi* might be translated " She is satisfied to unite nations and to make treaties " (Pl. XIX, 4).

The badge of *Barbados* represents Britannia, crowned and holding her trident, standing in a sea-shell and drawn by two sea-horses (Pl. XIX, 5).

The *Turks and Caicos Islands* shows on its badge a three-masted vessel lying off a stretch of shore on which a red-coated native is apparently making salt; nearby are two dome-shaped huts (Pl. XIX, 6).

The badge of the *Windward Islands* (Pl. XX, 2) shows a shield quartered red, yellow, green and  white, encircled by a garter surmounted by the Royal Crown and bearing the words " Governor in Chief, Windward Islands"; below a scroll bears the motto *I pede fausto* (" Go with a fortunate foot "). Three of the group's islands also have their own badges. That of *Dominica* shows a sailing-ship moored to a jetty; in the background the sun rises over the hills. That of *St. Lucia* is a shield quartering, by two lengths of bamboo, two roses with two fleurs-de-lis. That of *St. Vincent* shows two female figures at an altar, one holding an olive branch; the motto, *Pax et Justicia*, means " Peace and Justice ".

The ships represented on the badge of the *Leeward Islands* (Pl. XIX, 2) are surprisingly out of perspective. Above is the Royal Arms. In the foreground are one large pineapple and three small

64

ones, said to represent a former Governor of the Islands—Sir Benjamin Pine, designer of the badge—and his family! The badge of *Antigua*, one of the group's islands, represents a coastal scene. That of *Montserrat*, another island in the group, shows a female figure, robed in green, supported by a cross and touching a harp at its foot.

The badge of the *Bahamas* consists of a shield of arms; in the chief the Royal Crown on a red background and beneath a seascape on which three ships are sailing. The motto: *Commercia Expulsis Piratis Restituta* (" Commerce restored by the expulsion of the pirates ") (Pl. XX, 3). The badge of the *Virgin Islands* typifies its name: a white-robed figure holds an antique lamp: she stands between two vertical rows, one of five and one of six such lamps (Pl. XX, 4).

ELSEWHERE IN THE AMERICAS

The badge of *Bermuda* (Pl. XX, 5) is a shield on which appears a lion holding a smaller shield displaying the wreck of the *Sea Venture* in 1609.

British Honduras (Pl. XX, 6), in Central America, displays as its badge a shield with a scrolled edge, and divided into three segments ; these show the

British Union Flag, the tools used in felling mahogany, and a three-masted ship at sea.

The *Falkland Islands* are situated off the southern tip of South America. Their badge is a shield displaying a ram standing on a patch of tussac grass ; below this appears an heraldic sea on which is represented the ship *Desire*, by which the islands were discovered in 1592 ; this is referred to in the motto, " Desire the Right ".

The badge of *British Guiana*, on the mainland of South America, also shows a three-masted ship at sea, in full sail and wearing the Red Ensign ; a scroll bears the motto *Damus Petimusque Vicissim* (" We give and seek in turn ").

THE SOUTH SEAS

The *Protectorate of Tonga*, consisting of the Tongan or Friendly Islands, has several flags. The National Flag is red with a small white canton bearing a red Greek cross (with equal arms). The Standard of the Queen of Tonga, which places the red cross on a white six-pointed star at its centre, is quartered,

1. National Flag

2. Royal Standard

PLATE XXI. TONGA

yellow with three white stars, red with a crown proper, blue with a dove carrying an olive-branch in its beak, and yellow with three swords (Pl. XXI, 1, 2).

The badge of the *Fiji Islands* consists of the full Coat-of-Arms : the shield displays, gold on red, a lion holding a coco-pod between its fore-paws ; below this a St. George's Cross, red on white,

67

quarters three sugar canes, a coconut palm, a dove with a sprig of olive in its beak, and a bunch of bananas. The crest is a native canoe, and the

supporters are Fijians in native dress ; the motto *Rere Vaka na Kalou ka doka na Tui* is Fijian and means "Fear God and Honour the King".

The shield of the *British Solomon Islands* depicts a gold lion on a red field ; below this the shield is quartered blue and white, the four quarters bearing respectively an eagle, a turtle, a native shield with spears, and two flying birds, all in natural colours. That of the *Gilbert and Ellice Islands* displays a frigate bird, gold on red, against a background showing the sun rising over the sea. The smaller islands in the Pacific are supervised by the *Western Pacific High Commissioner*, who places on a white circle surrounded by a garland at the centre of the Union Flag the Royal Crown emblem above the letters "W.P.H.C."

THE MEDITERRANEAN

The badge of *Gibraltar*, the fortress which is " the key to the Mediterranean", depicts on an ornamental red shield a triple-towered castle above a gold key; the motto, *Montis Insignia Calpe* (" The Badge of Mount Calpe "), refers to the classical name of " the Rock " (Pl. XXII, 1).

The *Republic of Cyprus* uses a white flag bearing a map of the island, in old gold, with two sprigs of green leaves (Pl. XXII, 6).

The Badge of *Malta* was formerly a shield halved vertically, white and red; the Island Flag was halved similarly. In 1943, by a Royal Warrant authorised by King George VI, " to bear witness to the heroism and devotion of its people ", the island became Malta, G.C., and its badge and flag have since borne a small blue canton bearing the emblem, in natural colours, of the George Cross (Pl. XXII, 2).

THE INDIAN OCEAN

The badge of the *Seychelles* depicts a sandy sea-washed beach on which a turtle crawls under a palm tree; the motto is *Finis Coronat Opus* (" The finish crowns the work "). That of *Mauritius* is the island's Coat-of-Arms: on the quartered shield appear an antique galley, gold on blue, three palm-trees green on gold, a red key on gold, and a star above a triangle in white on blue; the supporters are a sambur and the extinct dodo, each holding a sugar-cane; the motto *Stella Clavisque Maris Indici* (" The Sign is a Star and the Key of the Sea ") refers to the island's claim to be at once the key and the star of the Indian Ocean. The badge of *Aden* displays, in white and green, a native

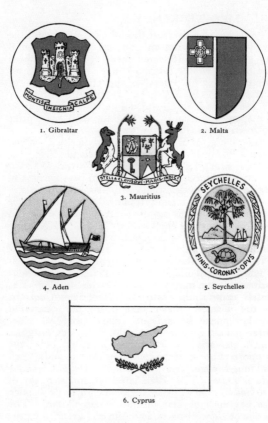

1. Gibraltar

2. Malta

3. Mauritius

4. Aden

5. Seychelles

6. Cyprus

PLATE XXII.

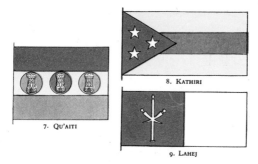

7. QU'AITI

8. KATHIRI

9. LAHEJ

PLATE XXIIa.   BRITISH PROTECTED STATES

boat with two sails sailing, against a blue sky, on an
heraldic sea of blue and white stripes (Pl. XXII,
3-5).

The National Flag of *Qu'aiti* (Pl. XXII, 7) is a
horizontal tricolour, red, yellow and blue; on the
central stripe three white towers are shown within
circles of blue, green and blue; the Sultan's
Standard displays an Eastern Crown, in gold, on the
upper stripe.   The National Flag of *Kathiri*
(Pl. XXII, 8) is a tricolour of yellow, green and
yellow: a red triangle in the hoist bears three white
stars; the Sultan's Standard displays a crown on the
central stripe.   The flag of the Sultanate of *Lahej*
is halved vertically, red and white; on the red half
appears a white silhouette of a sceptre and two
crossed daggers (Pl. XXII, 9).

THE UNITED STATES OF AMERICA

THE NATIONAL FLAG

The National Flag of the United States of America, which is also the Ensign and the Merchant Flag, is " The Star-Spangled Banner ", " Old Glory ", the " Stars and Stripes" (Pls. XXIII, XXIV).

The stars, white on blue, in the canton, represent the number of States forming the Union ; until recently this number stood at forty-eight, but in 1959, following the admission of Alaska as a state, it was increased to forty-nine, and in July 1960, following that of Hawaii, it became fifty, in nine alternate rows of six and five. The thirteen red and white stripes in the fly represent the original States from which the Union grew.

The U.S. Jack, sometimes called the " Union " and sometimes even the "Union Jack", is identical with the canton. The Warship Pennant bears seven stars, white on blue, at the head ; for the rest of its length it is divided horizontally, red over white, and it ends in a long " swallow-tail ".

The display of the Stars and Stripes is strictly regulated by the Flag Code. Except where for special reasons—as at the Capitol—it is kept flying day and night, it is flown only during the hours of daylight. Solely as a signal of dire distress is it to be inverted, and no other flag—except, during Divine Service, the Naval Church Pennant (a blue Latin Cross placed horizontally on a white field)—

may be flown above it. When it is ceremonially paraded or hoisted or lowered, all present must face it and stand to attention : those in uniform salute, others place the right hand over the heart, men holding the hat in the right hand. On suitable occasions the Pledge to the Flag is to be repeated :

" I pledge allegiance to the Flag of the United States of America, and to the Republic for which it stands, one nation under God, indivisible, with liberty and justice for all."

THE ORIGIN OF THE STARS AND STRIPES

When the American colonists rose in armed protest against the British Government, the emblem they first adopted signified both their unity and the loyalty which they still retained towards the Mother Country. Their *Great Union Flag*, also known as the Congress Flag and the Cambridge Flag, bore thirteen red and white stripes, but its canton was formed by the contemporary British Union Flag (Pl. XXIII, 2). This was also the flag of the East India Company, but whether it was deliberately adopted from this is unknown.

When, however, the Americans decided on a complete severance from Britain, they needed a new flag to symbolise their independence. While retaining the thirteen stripes in the fly, they replaced the Union in the canton by " thirteen stars white in a blue field representing a new constellation." The exact arrangement of the stars in the first American Flag is uncertain, but it is reputed to have been a circle so that one should have no precedence over the other (Pl. XXIII, 3).

As new States were admitted to the Union, the

1. National and Merchant Flag and Ensign (1959)

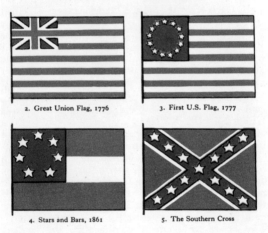

2. Great Union Flag, 1776

3. First U.S. Flag, 1777

4. Stars and Bars, 1861

5. The Southern Cross

PLATE XXIII. THE UNITED STATES OF AMERICA:
HISTORICAL FLAGS

1. National and Merchant Flag and Ensign

2. President's Standard

PLATE XXIV. THE UNITED STATES OF AMERICA

number of the stars and of the stripes was increased correspondingly. The increase in the number of stripes, however, threatened to destroy the flag's effectiveness. So, in 1818, Congress decided to revert to the original thirteen stripes but to signalise the admission of a new State by displaying an additional white star in the canton.

FLAGS OF THE CONFEDERATE STATES

During the Civil War the Southern Confederacy adopted a new flag which, while differing markedly from the Stars and Stripes, still generally resembled it in design. The *Stars and Bars* bore in its blue canton a circle of seven white stars symbolising the first States to secede from the Union, but merged the red and white of the fly into a bold tricolour (Pl. XXIII, 4).

This flag was found to resemble the Stars and Stripes too closely, and was therefore replaced by an emblem which retained the traditional American colours but arranged them very differently. The *Southern Cross*, the Confederate Battle Flag, displayed thirteen white stars on a blue saltire, fimbriated in white, on a red field (Pl. XXIII, 5). As this could not be inverted in case of need as a flag of distress, it later formed the canton of a flag with a white field; then, lest this be mistaken for a flag of truce, a broad red stripe was added down its fly.

THE PRESIDENT'S STANDARD

The Standard of the President of the United States is dark blue and bears, within a circle of stars, one for each state, a replica of the design on the Presidential Seal. The American Eagle is shown with its head turned towards its right talon, which holds an olive branch, while the left talon holds a bundle of arrows—the emblems of peace and war. Above and beside the head are thirteen white stars, representing the Founder States of the Union, and a scroll bears the motto *E Pluribus Unum*, " One out of Many " (Pl. XXIV).

FLAGS OF THE ARMED FORCES

The Flag of the U.S. Army is white with a gold fringe, and bears, in blue, the traditional emblems of freedom (Pl. XXV, 1).

The Standard of the U.S. Marine Corps, while original in design, shows the influence of the British tradition. Its emblem, as in the Colours of the Royal Marines, incorporates the foul anchor and the terrestrial globe—but naturally replaces the eastern hemisphere by the western. The globe is surmounted by the American Eagle, which holds in its beak a scroll bearing the Corps motto, *Semper Fidelis* ("Always Faithful"). The field is scarlet and the fringe gold, these being the Corps colours (Pl. XXV, 2).

In the individual units the methods of using distinguishing flags, though based on those of the British Army, depart from them in several respects. In all arms, the larger units bear two emblems, the National Colours consisting of the Stars and Stripes and the Regimental or other organisational Colours differing from unit to unit in their insignia. Each arm has its assigned colour-usage: infantry units, for example, place white insignia on a blue field. The smaller units have one flag only, a swallow-tailed guidon.

The Command Flags of the Senior officers indicate the rank by the number of white stars which they bear. In those of the U.S. Army the field is red; in those of the U.S. Navy and the U.S. Air Force the field is dark blue, but the arrangement of the stars is different. Those of the Navy are arranged vertically, or in a geometrical pattern; those of the Air Force are placed horizontally.

77

1. U.S. Army

2. U.S. Marine Corps

PLATE XXV. THE UNITED STATES ARMED FORCES

THE COASTGUARD AND CUSTOMS SERVICES

Unlike the National Flag, which is varied whenever a new State is admitted to the Union, the *U.S. Coastguard Ensign* has been altered very little since it was adopted over a century ago. Its sixteen vertical red and white stripes indicate the number of States in the Union when it was adopted; the

1. Coastguard Ensign

2. Yacht Ensign

Plate XXVI. United States Civil Ensigns

Eagle in the canton, dark blue on white, signifies Federal Service. The Coastguard badge in the fly includes a shield bearing thirteen white and red vertical stripes, two crossed anchors and the motto, *Semper Paratus* (" Always Prepared ") with the date 1790 (Pl. XXVI, 1). The Customs Service Ensign is similar but has no badge.

THE YACHT ENSIGN

Since 1848 Congress has authorised licensed yachts, those which conform to certain requirements, to wear a special *Yacht Ensign*. This resembles the original reputed Stars and Stripes in the number of stars in its canton as well as in its fly, but the circle of thirteen white stars in the canton surrounds a foul anchor, also in white, placed obliquely (Pl. XXVI, 2).

STATE FLAGS

All the States in the Union have their own flags (Pls. XXVII to XXXV). The designs are very varied ; many place the State Seal on a blue field, and a few have different emblems on the two sides. Some in the southern states show the influence of the Civil War ; others, formed out of the Louisiana purchase, that of France ; and others, that of European heraldry or the symbolism of native American peoples.

In spite of its colour, the flag of *Alabama*, officially described as " a crimson cross of St. Andrew on a white field", is said to be based on the Confederate Battle Flag.

Designed by a schoolboy, the flag of *Alaska* is simple but effective. Appropriately for so northerly a region, it displays the Great Bear constellation and the Pole Star (Pl. XXXV, 2).

The flag of *Arizona*, formerly that of the battleship named after the State, depicts the copper-coloured Star of Arizona before the setting sun ; it combines the State's colours with those of Imperial Spain.

The white stars on the blue border to the white lozenge on the flag of *Arkansas* indicate that it is the twenty-fifth State of the Union. The three stars below the name symbolise the three nations to which the region has belonged, Spain, France, and the U.S.A. ; that above the name commemorates the Confederacy.

The Bear Flag of *California*, dating from the time of the Western Pioneers, recalls the State's former existence as an independent republic.

The initial letter on the flag of *Colorado* surrounds a gold disc representing sunshine ; the tricolour symbolises the blue skies and the snow-capped mountains.

The State Seal on the light blue flag of *Connecticut*, an ornate gold-bordered shield displaying three grapevines, symbolises the three original colonies which formed the state. The motto, from the State's colonial banner, is *Qui Transtulit Sustenit* (" He who brought us over sustains us").

The buff diamond on the blue flag of *Delaware* bears the State Coat-of-Arms ; the date is that on which the State entered the Union. The buff colour may be derived from the insignia of the Netherlands, by whose people the region was colonised.

The flag of *Florida* resembles that of Alabama but at its centre is a reproduction of the State Seal. Prominent in the landscape which it depicts is an Indian woman scattering flowers, in reference to the State's name ; the motto is " In God we trust".

The flag of *Georgia* prominently displays the Battle Flag of the Confederacy. The broad blue stripe in the hoist bears a replica of the State Seal,

81

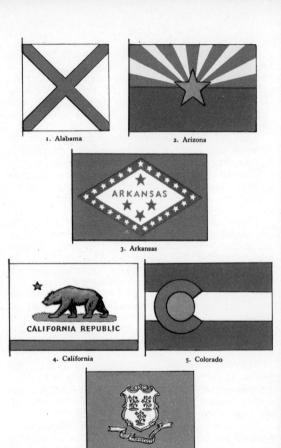

1. Alabama

2. Arizona

3. Arkansas

4. California

5. Colorado

6. Connecticut

PLATE XXVII. STATE FLAGS OF THE U.S.A.—(i)

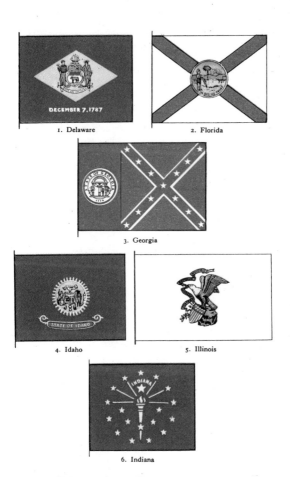

1. Delaware

2. Florida

3. Georgia

4. Idaho

5. Illinois

6. Indiana

PLATE XXVIII. STATE FLAGS OF THE U.S.A.—(ii)

on which three pillars engraved " Wisdom, Justice, Moderation ", for the legislative, judicial and executive branches of government, support an arch inscribed " Constitution ".

The canton of the flag of *Hawaii* is formed by the British Union Flag, thus recalling the discovery of the islands by Captain James Cook in 1778. In 1900 they were formally annexed by the United States. The white, red and blue stripes in the fly represent the eight islands in the group (Pl. XXXV, 3).

The State Coat-of-Arms of *Idaho* includes a shield showing the sun rising over the mountains ; the supporters are a woman with a spear and a pair of scales and wearing the cap of liberty, and a miner with a pick ; the crest is a moose's head and the motto *Esto Perpetua* (" May she endure forever").

The State Seal of *Illinois*, displayed on a white field, shows an eagle perched on a rock and holding in its beak a scroll with the motto, " State Sovereignty, National Union ".

The gold torch depicted on the flag of *Indiana* symbolises liberty and enlightenment. The stars surrounding it represent the original thirteen States, the five below the torch those which joined the Union before Indiana, and the large star is for Indiana itself—the nineteenth State to be admitted to the Union.

The flag of *Iowa*, a state formed out of the Louisiana purchase, is adapted from the French tricolour : on the broad central stripe is depicted a flying eagle bearing a scroll inscribed " Our liberties we prize and our rights we will maintain".

The seal of *Kansas* is shown surmounted by the

State's floral emblem, the sunflower. In the landscape which it depicts, the ploughman represents agriculture and the herd of buffaloes pursued by mounted Indians, like the "prairie schooners" (covered wagons), recalls the State's history. The stars show that it was the thirty-fourth State to enter the Union, and the motto is *Ad Astra per Aspera* ("Through difficulties to the stars").

On the State Seal of *Kentucky*, reproduced on the flag, two men are shown shaking hands as though to illustrate the motto, "United we stand, divided we fall". The wreath below the seal is formed of the State's flower, the goldenrod.

The emblem of *Louisiana*, white on a blue field, is the traditional symbol of devotion, a pelican feeding its young. A scroll below bears the words "Union, Justice, and Confidence".

The Coat-of-Arms of *Maine* appears on a blue flag. The shield depicts a moose lying at the foot of a pine tree; the supporters are a farmer with his scythe and a seaman with his anchor; above appears the North Star with the word *Dirigo* ("I direct").

The heraldic device on the quartered flag of *Maryland* dates from the founding of the colony early in the seventeenth century. It depicts the arms of Lord Baltimore, the colony's founder, quartering the Arms of his father (Calvert) with those of his mother (Crossland).

The State Seal shown on the obverse of the white flag of *Massachusetts* displays, beneath a gold star, an Indian armed with bow and arrow; the crest is an arm grasping a broadsword and the motto is *Ense Petit Placidam sub Libertate Quietem*

85

1. Iowa

2. Kansas

3. Kentucky

4. Louisiana

5. Maine

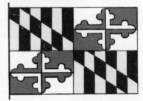

6. Maryland

PLATE XXIX. STATE FLAGS OF THE U.S.A.—(iii)

1. Massachusetts

2. Michigan

3. Minnesota

4. Mississippi

5. Missouri

6. Montana

PLATE XXX. STATE FLAGS OF THE U.S.A.—(iv)

("With the sword she seeks peace under liberty").
The reverse depicts a blue shield bearing a green
pine tree.

The word *Tuebor* ("I will defend") on the
Coat-of-Arms shown on the flag of *Michigan*
refers to the State's position on the Canadian
frontier; the device shows a man standing on a
headland lit by the rising sun. The supporters are
an elk and a moose, and the crest is formed by the
American eagle and motto. A scroll below bears
the command *Si Quaeris Peninsulam Amoenam
Circumspice* ("If you seek a beautiful peninsula,
look around you").

On the obverse of the flag of *Minnesota* the State
Seal is shown on a white field; the reverse of the
flag is blue. The device, a white farmer watching
an Indian horseman riding westwards, refers to the
spread of civilisation. The nineteen stars show
that this was the nineteenth State, after the original
thirteen, to be admitted to the Union; they are
arranged to form a larger star symbolising Minnesota as the "North Star State", as is expressed by
the words *L'Etoile du Nord*. The staff is surmounted
by that typical prairie animal, the gopher.

The Confederacy is recalled not only in the Battle
Flag, which forms the canton of the flag of
Mississippi, but in the tricolour fly, which suggests
the Stars and Bars; the colours are however blue,
white and red, possibly recalling the Louisiana
purchase.

The Louisiana purchase may also be responsible
for the tricolour flag of *Missouri*. This bears a
replica of the State Seal, surrounded by a circle of
stars which indicate that the State was the twenty-

fourth to join the Union. The two mottoes read
" United we stand, Divided we fall " and *Salus
Populi Suprema Lex Esto* (" The welfare of the
people is the supreme law ").

The State Seal on the blue flag of *Montana*,
which has a narrow gold fringe along its upper and
lower edges, depicts the sun setting behind mountains overlooking the Great Falls of the Missouri ;
in the foreground are a plough and a miner's pick
and shovel. The words *Oro y Plata* (" Gold and
Silver ") refer to the State's mineral wealth. This
flag resembles that carried by the Montana Infantry
in the Spanish-American War.

The State Seal of *Nebraska* shows a steamboat
ascending the Missouri, a train steaming towards the
Rockies, and—to represent the mechanical arts and
agriculture—a blacksmith and a settler's cabin.
The motto is " Equality before the law ".

The blue flag of *Nevada* displays in the canton
a silver star above a wreath of the State flower,
the sage-brush. The words " Battle Born " recall
that the State was admitted to the Union during
the Civil War.

The State Seal of *New Hampshire* is encircled by
a wreath of laurel interspersed with stars ; it
depicts the frigate *Raleigh*, one of the first vessels in
the American Navy.

The buff colour of the flag of *New Jersey* is that
of the facings of the State troops during the War
of Independence, and is said to have been chosen
by George Washington because it figured in the
insignia of the Netherlands. The flag depicts the
State Coat-of-Arms ; the supporters, female figures
bearing respectively a Cap of Liberty and a

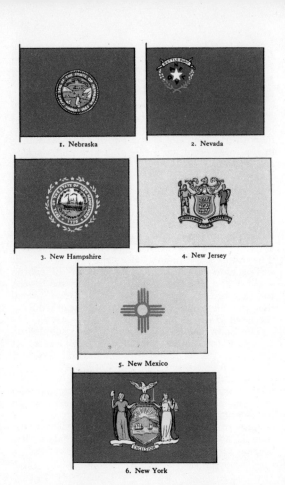

1. Nebraska

2. Nevada

3. New Hampshire

4. New Jersey

5. New Mexico

6. New York

PLATE XXXI. STATE FLAGS OF THE U.S.A.—(v)

1. North Carolina

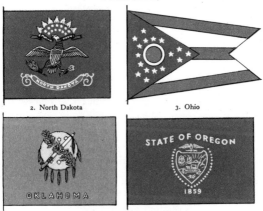

2. North Dakota

3. Ohio

4. Oklahoma

5. Oregon

6. Pennsylvania

PLATE XXXII. STATE FLAGS OF THE U.S.A.—(vi)

cornucopia, refer to the motto "Liberty and Prosperity".

On the yellow flag of *New Mexico* the ancient Zia sun-symbol of the Zuni Indians appears in red; these are the colours of Old Spain, which once ruled this region.

The flag of *New York State* boldly displays its Coat-of-Arms. The shield depicts a sloop and a ship under sail on the Hudson River; the crest is an eagle perched on part of the terrestrial globe showing the North Atlantic; the supporters are female figures representing Liberty and Justice, and the motto, *Excelsior*, hardly needs explanation.

The design of the civic flag of the *City of New York*—originally called "New Amsterdam"—commemorates the city's early history as a Dutch colony. A vertical tricolour, it bears in reverse the historic colours of the Netherlands, orange, white and blue. On the central stripe appears the city's seal: a saltire formed by the arms of a windmill

 quarters two beavers with two flour-barrels, symbolising New Amsterdam's chief articles of merchandise, fur and food; the crest resembles that of New York State, the supporters are a seaman holding navigational instruments and a Red Indian holding a bow; the motto is *Sigillum Civitate Novi Eboraci* ("The seal of the City of New York").

The flag of *North Carolina* recalls in its red and white fly the influence of the Stars and Bars; the dates on the royal blue stripe in the hoist are those of events significant in the State's history.

The design on the blue flag of *North Dakota*,

92

which includes the American eagle, the national motto, the thirteen white stars and the shield striped red and white, is based on that of the Regimental Colours of the First North Dakota Infantry in the Spanish-American War and the Phillippine Insurrection.

The State of *Ohio* flies not the usual rectangular flag but a tapering burgee of the national colours. The stars indicate that this was the seventeenth State to join the Union, and the red circle with the white border suggest both the State's initial letter and its unofficial name, the " Buckeye State ".

The device on the light blue flag of *Oklahoma* depicts an Indian warrior's rawhide shield, from which hang seven eagle's feathers. Upon the shield are crossed another Indian emblem, the *calumet* (pipe of peace) and the classical symbol of peace, the olive branch.

On the obverse of the flag of *Oregon* appears the shield from the State's Coat-of-Arms : it depicts a covered wagon on the shore of the Pacific Ocean, on which a British man-o'-war is departing and an American ship arriving ; and, below a scroll bearing the words "The Union", a sheaf, a plough, and a pickaxe; the crest is the American Eagle. On the reverse of the flag is portrayed a golden beaver.

The State Coat-of-Arms appears on the flag of *Pennsylvania*. The shield depicts a ship at sea, a plough, and three wheatsheaves ; the supporters are horses in harness and the crest is an eagle; the motto reads, "Virtue, Liberty and Independence".

The golden anchor displayed on the white flag of *Rhode Island* is the traditional symbol of hope ; the thirteen gold stars represent the original States of the Union.

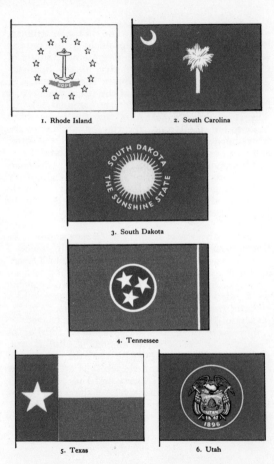

1. Rhode Island

2. South Carolina

3. South Dakota

4. Tennessee

5. Texas

6. Utah

PLATE XXXIII. STATE FLAGS OF THE U.S.A.—(vii)

1. Vermont

2. Virginia

3. Washington

4. West Virginia

5. Wisconsin

6. Wyoming

PLATE XXXIV. STATE FLAGS OF THE U.S.A.—(viii)

The flag of *South Carolina* is based on what is traditionally the first American flag displayed in the Southern States during the War of Independence : the *Moultrie Flag*, blue with a white crescent moon in the upper hoist ; the white palm-tree was added when the State seceded at the beginning of the Civil War.

The golden sun on the obverse of the blue flag of *South Dakota* refers to its claim to be the " Sunshine State ". On the reverse appears the State Seal, depicting hills, a steamboat on a river, a farmer with his plough, a field of corn, and a smelting furnace with the motto " Under God the people rule ".

The flag of *Tennessee* displays the national colours : the three stars show that it was the third State to be admitted into the Union after the original thirteen.

The flag of *Texas* is that used during the State's independence. Its general design almost suggests that the Stars and Bars was derived from it, but the resemblance may be coincidental. The emblem in the hoist typifies the " Lone Star State ".

Surrounded by a narrow gold ring, the State Seal appears on the flag of *Utah*. The shield displays a beehive, the emblem of industry, and the State's flower, the sego lily; the crest is the American Eagle, and the usual supporters are replaced by two American Flags. The dates are those on which the State was founded by the Mormons, who called it *Deseret* (Land of the Honey Bee) and of its admission to the Union.

The flag of *Vermont* shows the State's Coat-of-Arms. The landscape depicted on the shield includes a pine-tree, three wheatsheaves and a red cow, with a mountain range in the background. The motto is " Freedom and Unity ".

The State Seal depicted on the flag of *Virginia*, which is blue with a narrow gold stripe down its fly, dates almost from the Declaration of Independence. It shows Virtue, dressed like an Amazon and armed with sword and spear, trampling down the figure of Tyranny, whose crown is fallen and who grasps a broken chain and a whip. The motto is *Sic Semper Tyrannis* ("Thus ever to Tyrants ").

The green flag of the *State of Washington* bears a replica of the State Seal : within a gold circle appear the head and shoulders of George Washington, after whom the State was named.

The white blue-bordered flag of *West Virginia* shows the State's Coat-of-Arms. The shield depicts a rock beside which stand a farmer and a miner with implements symbolising the clearing of the forests, agriculture, and the mechanical arts ; two crossed rifles are surmounted by the Cap of Liberty ; the motto is *Montani Semper Liberi* (" Mountaineers always free ").

The State Coat-of-Arms appears on the square flag of *Wisconsin*. The shield quarters a plough, a crossed shovel and pick, an arm brandishing a hammer, and an anchor ; the supporters are a seaman and a labourer, the crest is the State animal, a beaver, and the motto is " Forward ".

The flag of *Wyoming* displays the national colours and bears in white the silhouette of a buffalo ; on its side appears the State Seal.

1. District of Columbia

2. State of Alaska

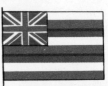

3. State of Hawaii

4. Governor of the Panama Canal Zone

5. Governor of Guam

6. Puerto Rico

7. Virgin Islands

PLATE XXXV.   U.S. STATE FLAGS, DISTRICTS,
TERRITORIES AND DEPENDENCIES

OTHER U.S. FLAGS

Based on George Washington's Shield of Arms, which is doubtfully reputed to have influenced the design of the U.S. National Flag, the white flag of the *District of Columbia* depicts three red stars over two horizontal red stripes (Pl. XXXV, 1).

The dark blue flags of the Governors of the *Panama Canal Zone* and of *Guam* depict the respective Seals (Pl. XXXV, 4, 5). That of Panama is a shield displaying a Spanish galleon sailing between two cliffs ; above are thirteen white and red vertical stripes and below appears the motto " The land divided, the world united ". The seal of Guam shows a coconut tree growing beside an estuary on which sails an outrigger canoe.

The white flag of the *Virgin Islands* displays the American Eagle between the two letters " V " and " I ". (Pl. XXXV, 7).

The flag of *Puerto Rico* is that borne by its people when with the people of Cuba they revolted against Spanish rule : five red and white horizontal stripes with a blue triangle displaying a white star in the hoist (Pl. XXXV, 6). The Governor's flag is white and bears a replica of the Island's seal.

THE WESTERN POWERS

The problems arising from the Second World War have caused the formation of several international organisations which link the United States with Western Europe. Some of these organisations have their own distinguishing flags.

The green flag of the *Supreme Headquarters Allied Powers in Europe* (S.H.A.P.E.) signifies the woodlands and fields of Europe. It displays the Organisation's insignia, a green silver-edged shield depicting two golden swords forming the letter "A", twelve silver fronds representing the original signatories of N.A.T.O. and two olive sprays signifying N.A.T.O.'s dedication to peace (Pl. XXXVI, 2).

The flag of N.A.T.O. itself, the *North Atlantic Treaty Organisation*, is dark blue, suggestive of the Atlantic Ocean, and is charged in white with a compass rose (to indicate that N.A.T.O.'s work is directed towards world peace) within a white circle signifying unity; the colours are those of the Organisation (Pl. XXXVI, 1).

The *Consultative Assembly of the Council of Europe* flies a blue flag depicting a circle of twelve gold five-pointed stars, one for each of the nations represented in the Assembly (Pl. XXXVI, 3).

The *United Europe* flag—that of the *Mouvement Européen*—consists of a gigantic letter " E " in green on a white flag.

EUROPE

EIRE. The National Flag, Ensign and Merchant Flag of the Republic of Ireland (Eire) is a vertical tricolour of green, white and orange (Pl. XXXVII, 1). This emblem is over a hundred years old, having been borne by the Irish Nationalists' organisations at least as early as 1830, and its design was probably suggested by the French tricolour which, as the symbol of a successful revolution, commended itself to such bodies ; indeed the two flags are said to have been sometimes flown side by side. In adopting the French flag, the Irish substituted their own traditional colours, green for the " Emerald Isle", orange for the Ulstermen of the North (and to recall their hero, William of Orange), and white to symbolise the peace and unity which, it was hoped, would prevail between them.

The Easter Rising of 1916 converted this flag into a national emblem ; it was adopted officially when the Irish Free State was constituted in 1921; and its use was continued when in 1937 the State finally achieved independence as the Republic of Ireland. Its design and display is governed by a set of rules apparently based on the Flag Code of the U.S.A.

Another traditional emblem, the Irish harp, gold on a green field, which had formerly been the national flag, now forms the Jack. The President's Flag displays the golden harp on a blue field (Pl. XXXVII, 2).

1. N.A.T.O.

2. S.H.A.P.E.

3. Consultative Assembly of the Council of Europe

PLATE XXXVI. THE WESTERN POWERS

1. National and Merchant Flag and Ensign

2. President's Flag

PLATE XXXVII. EIRE

FRANCE. The flag of France is the famous
Tricolour, striped vertically blue, white and red
(Pl. XXXVIII, 1). On the National Flag the stripes
are of equal width ; but as, owing to differences in
visibility of the three colours, they never look equal
from a distance, this is compensated for on the
Ensign, Merchant Flag and Jack by making the
white stripe slightly wider than the blue, and the
red a little wider still.

The Tricolour may have been adopted from the
somewhat similar flag of the Netherlands, itself
the emblem of a successful revolution. It also

combined the colours of the city of Paris, red and blue, with that of the Bourbon monarchy, white—though the traditional emblem of the monarchy, the lilies of France, dropped out of use.

The President's Flag is a square tricolour and bears his initials on the centre stripe. Similar tricolours with distinguishing emblems form the Command and other official flags.

Vessels which during the recent war served in the Free French Naval Forces commemorate this service by wearing a special Jack. This rearranges the national colours as a large white diamond on a flag blue in the hoist and red in the fly; at the centre of the diamond is the red Cross of Lorraine, the wartime emblem of the Free French Forces (Pl. XXXVIII, 2).

MONACO. The National Flag of Monaco is halved horizontally, red over white. The Prince's Standard displays the Royal Arms on a white field.

BELGIUM. The flag of Belgium is a vertical tricolour, black, gold and red; the National Flag is almost square (Pl. XXXIX, 1), the Merchant Flag is rectangular. This is another revolutionary emblem, having been borne by the people of Brabant when they revolted against the Austrians in 1787, and this Brabancon flag became the national emblem of Belgium when it achieved independence in 1830.

The Ensign arranges the national colours as a gold saltire, bordered by red above and below and by black towards the hoist and fly, on a white field. Above the saltire a crown surmounts two crossed cannon, in black, and below it is a black foul anchor (Pl. XXXIX, 3).

The Royal Standard (Pl. XXXIX, 2)—used only afloat, and in miniature as the King's car flag—is square. The Royal Arms, a gold lion rampant on a black shield surmounted by a crown, appear on a dark red field ; in each corner appears the initial of the King. Other personal Standards bear the respective initials of the Queen, or any other *male* member of the Royal Family, also ensigned with a crown.

The Belgian Air Force Ensign is air-force blue with a large target, a black disc surrounded by circles of gold and red fimbriated with gold, at its centre. In the upper hoist the shield ensigned with the crown and charged with a gold lion is superimposed upon a pair of stylised wings (Pl. XXXIX, 4).

LUXEMBURG. The National Flag of the Grand Duchy of Luxemburg is similar to that of the Netherlands, but differs somewhat from this in length and in one of its colours : a horizontal tri-colour of red, white, and a lighter blue.

The Standard of the Grand Duchess places the Royal Arms on the obverse only of the National Flag. The shield quarters the lion rampant and billets of Nassau, gold on a blue field, with the lion rampant of Luxemburg, red on a field consisting of nine horizontal white and blue stripes ; it is ensigned with the grand-ducal crown, and the supporters are two crowned rampant lions in gold (Pl. XXXVIII, 3).

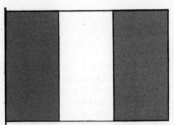

FRANCE. I. National and Merchant Flag, Ensign and Jack

2. Free French Jack

3. LUXEMBURG. Standard of Grand Duchess

PLATE XXXVIII

1. National Flag

2. Royal Standard

3. Ensign

4. Air Force Ensign

PLATE XXXIX. BELGIUM

THE NETHERLANDS. The National Flag, Ensign and Merchant Flag of the Netherlands (Holland) is a horizontal tricolour of red, white and blue. (Pl. XL, 1). Its colours were orginally orange, white and blue, those of the Prince of Orange, and under his leadership it became a banner of revolt when the Netherlands rose in armed resistance to the rule of Spain ; it thus set a tradition, which has endured to our own times, of using a tricolour as a revolutionary emblem.

On Royal anniversaries and other days of national rejoicing loyal Netherlanders may add an orange fly to their tricolour or hoist an orange pendant above it.

The Jack arranges the national colours alternately in a series of twelve triangles meeting at the flag's centre (Pl. XL, 4).

The Royal Standard of the Queen of the Netherlands is orange ; a blue cross of St. George type quarters four blue bugle-horns, and at its centre is the Royal Shield ensigned with a crown and displaying a gold lion rampant on a blue field. The Standard of Prince Bernhard bears an orange cross which quarters two lions rampant, gold on blue, with two roses, red and gold on white ; at its centre is a simpler version of the Royal Shield with its crown (Pl. XL, 2, 3).

The Royal Dutch Air Force Ensign is light blue; an orange isosceles triangle with its base at the hoist and its apex at the fly extends across it and on this appears the badge of the Military Order of William, 4th Class,

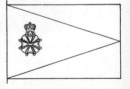

the highest Dutch award "for gallantry, conduct and faithfulness" in battle.

WEST GERMANY. The National and Merchant Flag of the West German Federal Republic is a horizontal tricolour of black, red and gold. (Pl. XLI, 1). These were the colours adopted by the Weimar Republic constituted after the First World War. The Government Authorities Flag places a shield displaying an eagle, black on gold, a little to the hoist side of the centre; the Ensign and Jack are similar but have swallow-tails. The Post Office Flag depicts a post-horn on the centre stripe, which is slightly widened to accommodate it.

The President's Flag is square and displays the eagle, in black, on a gold field with a red border (Pl. XLI, 2).

EAST GERMANY. The National and Merchant Flag of the East German Democratic Republic is similar to that of the Federal Republic, the horizontal tricolour of black, red and gold, but bears the State Emblem in the centre (Pl. XLI, 4).

The President's Flag is square ; on a red field, with a narrow edging of gold and red, it displays the State Emblem. This depicts, in gold, a pair of dividers superimposed on a hammer, possibly representing "the workers with hand and brain", within a wreath of ears of corn also in gold and tied with a black, red and gold ribbon (Pl. XLI, 3).

DENMARK. The flags of the Scandinavian countries display a cross of the St. George type, but with its upright slightly towards the hoist. The National and Merchant Flag of Denmark is the

1. National and Merchant Flag and Ensign

2. Royal Standard

3. Prince Bernhard's Standard

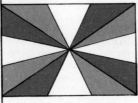

4. Jack

PLATE XL. NETHERLANDS

1. W. German National and Merchant Flag

2. W. German President

3. E. German President

4. E. German State Flag

PLATE XLI. GERMANY

reverse of the English flag, a white cross on a red field (Pl. XLII, 1). This flag, the *Dannebrog* ("Strength of Denmark") was according to tradition suggested by a vision beheld in the sky by King Waldemar just before a battle in 1219, and is probably the oldest of the world's flags. The Ensign and Jack are similar but are swallow-tailed.

The Royal Standard places the Royal Coat-of-Arms on a white square at the centre of the cross on the Ensign. The Standards of the Queen and the Crown Prince similarly place simplified versions of the Arms.

FINLAND. The Merchant Flag of Finland displays a light blue cross on a white field (Pl. XLII, 3). The National Flag shows at the centre of the cross a red, gold-bordered shield depicting the National Arms, a rampant lion in gold brandishing a sword and trampling on a scimitar; the Ensign resembles this but ends in a swallow-tail of three points. The President's Flag shows in the canton of the Ensign a light blue cross with arms tapering towards the centre charged with a gold swastika. The Jack is square and shows the shield with its emblem in the centre of a white field.

ICELAND. The National and Merchant Flags of Iceland are blue and bear a red cross fimbriated in white (Pl. XLII, 2). The Government Flag and

Ensign are longer and end in a swallow-tail. The President's Flag places on a white blue-bordered square at the centre of the cross on the Ensign the National Arms : a shield displaying the white-bordered red cross on the blue field held on a fragment of stratified rock by the island's traditional " guardian spirits ", a bull, a vulture, a dragon and a giant.

THE FAROE ISLANDS. The National and Merchant Flag of the Faroe Islands is white and depicts a red cross fimbriated with blue (Pl. XLII, 4).

NORWAY. The flags of Norway resemble the *Dannebrog* with the addition of a blue cross along the mid-line of the white. The National and Merchant Flag is thus a blue cross, fimbriated in white, on a red field (Pl. XLIII, 1). The Ensign and Government Flag resemble it, but end in a three-pointed swallow-tail ; the Jack also resembles it but is square.
  The Royal Standard displays the National Arms, a crowned rampant lion grasping the battle-axe of St. Olave, all in gold on a red field (Pl. XLIII, 2).

SWEDEN. The National and Merchant Flag of Sweden displays a gold cross on a light blue field (Pl. XLIII, 4). The Ensign and Jack are similar but end in a swallow-tail of three points. The Royal Standards of the King and Queen are similarly swallow-tailed and show the " Great Coat-of-Arms " on a white square at the centre of the cross (Pl. XLIII, 3) ; those of other members of the Royal Family place in the same position a

H

1. DENMARK. National and Merchant Flag   2. ICELAND. National and Merchant Flag

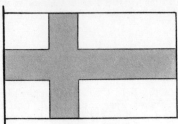

3. FINLAND. Merchant Flag

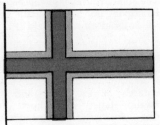

4. FAROE ISLANDS. National and Merchant Flag

PLATE XLII

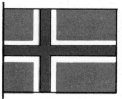

NORWAY. 1. National
and Merchant Flag

2. Royal Standard

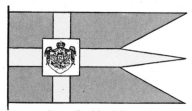

3. SWEDEN. Royal Standard

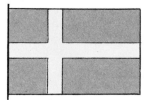

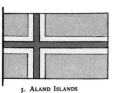

5. ALAND ISLANDS

4. SWEDEN. National and Merchant Flag

PLATE XLIII

115

smaller and simpler emblem displaying three golden crowns on a blue circle ensigned with the Royal Crown.

Each of the Royal Swedish Air Force wings has its own Colour. That shown belongs to a fighter wing: on a field of air force blue appear, in gold, a pair of conventionalised wings and a tractor screw ensigned by the Royal Crown; at the top of the hoist are a winged lion and four roses.

THE ALAND ISLANDS. The flag of the Aland (or Aaland) Islands is light blue and displays a red cross fimbriated in yellow (Pl. XLIII, 5).

SWITZERLAND. In contrast with the tricolours flown by the adjacent countries, the flags of Switzerland display a Greek Cross (with equal arms), white on a red field: the National Flag is square (Pl. XLIV, 1), the Merchant Flag rectangular. Like the tricolour, however, this flag is the emblem of a successful revolution, and dates from the fourteenth century when the Swiss of the mountain valleys revolted against their oppressive rulers ; they felt their cause to be as sacred as the Crusades, thus justifying the adoption of the Crusader's emblem.

The twenty-two Swiss cantons have their own flags, mostly consisting of simple designs in two or three colours.

AUSTRIA. The National and Merchant Flag of Austria is a horizontal tricolour, red, white and red (Pl. XLIV, 2). The State Flag displays on the central stripe the Arms of the Republic, a shield of the national colours, superimposed upon a black eagle crowned and grasping in talons from which hang broken fetters a hammer and a sickle. The design of the National Flag commemorates the prowess of Leopold Heldenthum, a mediaeval hero who battled so furiously that, except where it had been covered by his sword-belt, his white surcoat was stained with blood.

LIECHTENSTEIN. The National Flag of Liechtenstein is halved horizontally, royal blue and red ; on the blue stripe near the hoist is a crown (Pl. XLIV, 4). This was formerly shown with its base towards the fly, so that it was seen in its correct position when the flag was hung vertically, as from a horizontal staff. The Royal Flag is also halved horizontally, but its colours are those of the ruling dynasty, yellow and red.

HUNGARY. The National Flag of the People's Republic of Hungary is a horizontal tricolour of

1. SWITZERLAND. National Flag

2. AUSTRIA. National and Merchant Flag

3. HUNGARY. National Flag

4. LIECHTENSTEIN. National Flag

PLATE XLIV

118

red, white and green; the State
Emblem appears on the central
stripe. The tricolour flag dates
from the beginning of the seventeenth century (Pl. XLIV, 3).

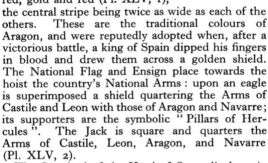

SPAIN. The Merchant Flag of
Spain is a horizontal tricolour,
red, gold and red (Pl. XLV, 1),
the central stripe being twice as wide as each of the
others. These are the traditional colours of
Aragon, and were reputedly adopted when, after a
victorious battle, a king of Spain dipped his fingers
in blood and drew them across a golden shield.
The National Flag and Ensign place towards the
hoist the country's National Arms : upon an eagle
is superimposed a shield quartering the Arms of
Castile and Leon with those of Aragon and Navarre;
its supporters are the symbolic " Pillars of Hercules ". The Jack is square and quarters the
Arms of Castile, Leon, Aragon, and Navarre
(Pl. XLV, 2).

The Standard of the Head of State displays, in
gold on a square red field the heads of two " wolf
dragons", facing each other diagonally across the
flag ; in each of the opposite corners appears one of
the " Pillars of Hercules " (Pl. XLV, 3).

The Command and other official flags place
distinguishing emblems on the tricolour. The Air
Force Ensign places the National Arms on the
central stripe with the word "Aviacion " beneath ;
on the upper stripe the black eagle appears on a red
disc ensigned with a naval crown and flanked by
silver wings.

ANDORRA Situated between France and Spain, Andorra uses in its National Flag, a tricolour of blue, gold and red colours adopted from its neighbours. The Flag may be either vertical or horizontal, and may display on its central stripe either a coronet or a quartered Shield (Pl. XLV, 4).

PORTUGAL. The flags of Portugal differ completely from the tricolour pattern typical of the greater part of Europe. The National Flag, Ensign and Merchant Flag is divided vertically, green in the hoist and red in the fly, the red being half as broad again as the green. Centred on the dividing line, the Arms of the former Monarchy are superimposed upon a gold armillary sphere, an astronomical instrument formerly much used by navigators. This is presumably a reference to the Portuguese voyages of discovery. The Arms consist of a white shield placed in the centre of a larger red shield, which surrounds it with seven golden castles ; five blue shields are arranged on the white shield to form a cross, and each of these shields bears five white roundels forming a saltire (Pl. XLVI, 1). The white shields commemorate the victory won in 1139 over five Moorish princes by Alfonso Henriquez at the battle of Ourique, a victory that made him the first king of Portugal ; he placed the five roundels upon them in reverence to the five wounds of Christ, in whose name he had defeated the Moslem invaders.

The Jack displays the same emblem at the centre of a square flag, red with a green border (Pl. XLVI, 2). It also appears centred on a green field to form the President's Flag (Pl. XLVI, 3);

the flags of Ministers place it at the intersection of a green saltire on a white field. It does not figure on the Command and other Flags, which place a green cross of St. George pattern on a white field, distinguishing emblems being added in the canton or at the centre of the cross (Pl. XLVI, 4).

ITALY. The National Flag of Italy is a vertical tricolour of green, white and red (Pl. XLVII, 1). Its identity, save for the colour of the stripe in its fly, with the French tricolour derives from its original use as the banner of the French Italian Legion during the campaign of 1796, and it was reputedly designed by Napoleon himself. To avoid confusion with the Merchant Flag of Mexico, that of Italy shows on the central stripe a shield encircled by a rope border and quartering the Arms of Venice (the Lion of St. Mark), Genoa, Amalfi, and Pisa. The shield on the Ensign differs very slightly from that on the Merchant Flag in detail and is surmounted by a crown of unusual design, a "towered and rostral" or "turreted crown", said to be based upon the *Corona Navalis* of Ancient Rome (Pl. XLVII, 2). The Jack is square ; its quarterings are similar to those on the shield of the Ensign but it has no rope border (Pl. XLVII, 3).

The President has no distinctive Flag of Office, his emblem being the National Flag.

SAN MARINO. The National Flag of San Marino is divided horizontally, white over blue, and

1. SPAIN. Merchant Flag

SPAIN. 2. Jack

3. Head of State

4. ANDORRA. National Flag

PLATE XLV

1. National and Merchant Flag and Ensign

2. Jack

3. President's Flag

4. Chief of the Navy

PLATE XLVI. PORTUGAL

123

bears at its centre the National Arms : within a wreath of oak and laurel and surmounted by a crown appear three mountain-peaks, supposedly those of Mount Titano, each bearing a white tower topped by a white ostrich feather. The Merchant Flag omits the arms.

TRIESTE. The flag of the Free Port of Trieste displays at the centre of a red field the silhouette of a halberd-head in white.

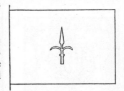

VATICAN CITY. Not only the headquarters of the Roman Catholic Church but a sovereign state in its own right, the Vatican City has its own National Flag. Based on the former emblem of the mediaeval papal States, this is halved vertically and contravenes strict heraldic procedure by its colours, gold in the hoist and white in the fly ; according to tradition, these colours were those of the banner borne in the Crusades by Godfrey of Jerusalem. In the fly appear, in gold, the Papal Emblem, the Triple Crown surmounting the Keys of St. Peter, one silver and one gold, crossed to form a saltire (Pl. XLVII, 4).

POLAND. The National Flag of Poland is halved horizontally, white above red (Pl. XLVIII, 2).

The Merchant Flag places in the centre of the upper half the National Arms, an eagle, white on a red shield with a decorative border (Pl. XLVIII, 1). The Ensign resembles the National Flag but is longer in proportion to its breadth and ends in a swallow-tail. The Jack bears the National Arms on a white field with a red border (Pl. XLVIII, 3).

The President's Flag shows the eagle on a red field with an ornamental border in red and white (Pl. XLVIII, 4).

CZECHOSLOVAKIA. The greater part of the National and Merchant Flag of Czechoslovakia is also halved horizontally red over white, but it is distinguished from the National Flag of Poland by a blue equilateral triangle in the hoist (Pl. XLVIII, 5). This emblem combines the colours of Bohemia, red and white, with that of Moravia, blue. The Ensign of the Czechoslovakian Armed Forces shows in the upper hoist a red pointed star, fimbriated in white where necessary to separate it from the blue triangle, and displaying the white lion rampant of Bohemia, wearing a gold coronet and having a double tail.

The President's Flag depicts on a white flag with an ornamental border of the national colours the Czechoslovakian Coat-of-Arms (Pl. XLVIII, 6).

RUMANIA. The Merchant Flag of the Rumanian People's Republic is a vertical tricolour of blue, gold and red. The National Flag and Ensign places the State Emblem on the middle stripe (Pl. XLIX, 1): it depicts a forest, with mountains over which the sun is rising; it is encircled by a wreath of wheat-ears tied with a ribbon of the national colours

1. ITALY. National Flag

2. ITALY. Ensign

3. ITALY. Jack

4. VATICAN CITY

PLATE XLVII
126

2. National Flag

POLAND. 1. Merchant Flag

POLAND. 3. Jack

4. President's Flag

CZECHOSLOVAKIA.
5. National and Merchant Flag

6. President's Flag

PLATE XLVIII

127

bearing the letters "R.P.R." —Republicii Populare Române; above is a gold-bordered red star. The Ensign shows the State Emblem on a white flag with a broad blue stripe along its lower edge; the Jack is square and displays the emblem at the centre of a broad red saltire fimbriated in gold on a blue field.

BULGARIA. The National and Merchant Flag of the People's Republic of Bulgaria (Pl. XLIX, 2) is a horizontal tricolour of white, green and red, typifying the love of peace, agriculture, and the bravery and endurance of the army. On the upper stripe, near the hoist, appears the State Arms, a golden lion rampant above a wheel, encircled with a wreath of wheatears tied with a ribbon of the national colours and surmounted by a red star. In the Ensign a small canton displays the lion; below is a red star on a white field; the rest of the flag consists of the tricolour. The Jack is square, with a red cross over a green saltire on a white field.

YUGOSLAVIA. Uniting the colours of Serbia and Montenegro, the National Flag and Merchant Flag of the Federal People's Republic of Yugoslavia are made up of a horizontal tricolour of blue, white and red, bearing at the centre a large five pointed red star fimbriated with gold; the National Flag is longer than the Merchant Flag (Pl. XLIX, 3). The Ensign is red and places the Merchant Flag in the canton with a golden wreath round the star. The Jack and Fortress Flag display on a red field the National Arms, five flaming torches within a wreath of golden ears of corn and surmounted by a star.

The flag of the Chief of Defence places the Ensign in the canton of a red flag with an ornamental red and gold border (Pl. XLIX, 4).

The State Flags of Serbia and Montenegro, of Croatia, and of Slovenia resemble the National Flag except for the order of the colours : respectively red, blue and white ; red, white and blue ; and white, blue and red. That of Bosnia and Herzegovina is red, and places the National Flag, fimbriated in white, in the canton. That of Macedonia is red, with the red gold-fimbriated star in the upper hoist.

ALBANIA. The National Flag of Albania is red, and displays at its centre the National Emblem, a black double-headed eagle with a red star above it fimbriated in gold (Pl. L, 1) ; this dates from Scanderbeg, the fifteenth century national patriot. The Merchant Flag is a horizontal tricolour, red, black and red, with a red star fimbriated in gold on the central stripe (Pl. L, 2).

GREECE. Of the two National Flags of Greece, that flown at sea, at the seaports and abroad (this is also the Merchant Flag) places in the canton a white Greek Cross on a blue field ; the fly consists of nine horizontal blue and white stripes (Pl. L, 3), standing by tradition for the nine syllables of the

1. RUMANIA. National Flag and Ensign

2. BULGARIA. National and Merchant Flag

YUGOSLAVIA.   3. Merchant Flag

4. Chief of Defence

PLATE XLIX

130

ALBANIA. 1. National Flag

2. Merchant Flag

GREECE. 3. Merchant Flag
and National Flag (at sea)

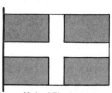

4. National Flag (on land)

GREECE. 5. Royal Standard

6. Jack

PLATE L

national motto, *Eleutheria a thanatos* (" Freedom
or death "). The other National Flag, flown only
within the country, is simply the white cross on the
blue field (Pl. L, 4).

A crown placed at the centre of the inland
National Flag converts it into the Fort or Service
Flag ; placed at the centre of the cross on the
maritime National Flag, it converts it into the
Ensign. The square Jack depicts a crown on the
centre of a white cross on a blue field (Pl. L, 6).

The Civil Air Ensign places on the centre of the
inland National Flag a target of blue, white and
blue ; the Air Force Ensign adds a gold crown
within a white circle in the canton.

The Royal Standard dis-
plays the Royal Arms at the
centre of a broad white cross
on a rectangular blue field
(Pl. L, 5). The King's Personal Standard places a
different version of the
Royal Arms at the centre of
a broad white cross quartering four crowns on a square
blue field ; the Crown
Prince's Standard is similar
but has a Crown only in the
canton ; the Queen's Personal Standard bears the
broad white cross on a rectangular blue field with
the Royal Arms both in the hoist and in the fly.

THE UNION OF SOVIET SOCIALIST
REPUBLICS

Unlike the opening stages of the American War

of Independence, the Bolshevist Revolution of 1917 in Russia meant a complete and immediate break with the national traditions of the past ; hence it demanded an entirely new emblem.

The Communist Party, by which the revolution was accomplished, had of course used the traditional symbol of revolution, the Red Flag. Hitherto, under the Czarist Government, it could be treasured only in secret ; now it could be displayed in triumph openly. What other flag could the Party adopt than the one which they had so long honoured and under which they had made their plans and dared arrest?

It needed, however, to be distinguished by a special national emblem. This does not form a canton but is displayed near the top of the hoist : below a star, the traditional symbol of authority, outlined in gold, there appear a crossed hammer and sickle, also in gold, symbols respectively of the industrial and agricultural workers, the inhabitants of town and country. This forms the State Flag and Merchant Flag of the Union of Soviet Socialist Republics (Pl. LI, 1).

The Ensign depicts the Red Star in the hoist, and the crossed hammer and sickle, in red, in the fly of a white flag with a light blue stripe along its lower edge (Pl. LI, 2). The Jack is red and displays a large white star ; within this is a smaller red star, at the centre of which appear the crossed hammer and sickle in white (Pl. LI, 3).

Most of the other flags of the Soviet Union also use the star and the crossed hammer and sickle variously arranged. Several resemble the Ensign but are distinguished by special symbols, and the

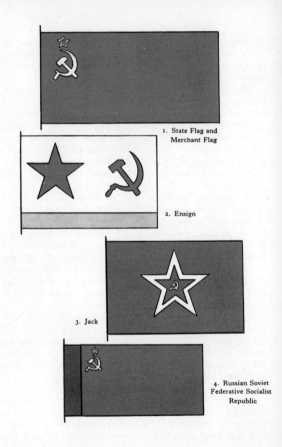

1. State Flag and
   Merchant Flag

2. Ensign

3. Jack

4. Russian Soviet
   Federative Socialist
   Republic

PLATE LI. UNION OF SOVIET SOCIALIST REPUBLICS

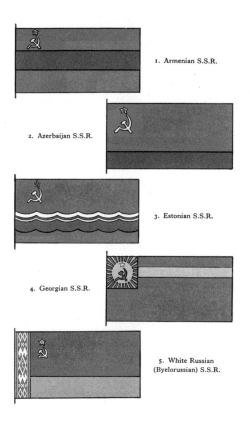

1. Armenian S.S.R.

2. Azerbaijan S.S.R.

3. Estonian S.S.R.

4. Georgian S.S.R.

5. White Russian (Byelorussian) S.S.R.

PLATE LII. THE SOVIET SOCIALIST REPUBLICS—(i)

Ensign itself occupies the canton of a number of others ; in the Command Flags the field is red.

The flag of the Soviet Air Force is distinctive ; on a light blue flag, with a narrow gold stripe down its fly, there appears, in gold, the sun emitting fourteen rays. The crossed hammer and sickle emblem, in gold, is placed at the centre of a red star depicted on the sun. Immediately below the sun a pair of stylised wings are ensigned upon a black aeroplane tractor-screw.

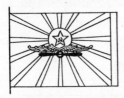 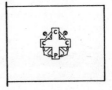

The Sea Rescue Flag is exceptional in that it does not bear either of the Soviet emblems—perhaps because of its reputed derivation from the flag of the Latvian Lifeboat Society, itself suggested by that of the Finnish Sea Saving Society. It resembles the Red Cross Flag but the cross is superimposed upon two blue anchors in saltire, and bears on each of its arms one of the letters " C.C.C.P."—the initials in the Cyrillic alphabet of the U.S.S.R.

THE CONSTITUENT SOVIET REPUBLICS

Each of the Soviet Republics which constitute the Union has its own flag. The field of all of these is predominantly red, and each places the star and the crossed hammer and sickle near the top of the hoist ; with one exception these resemble those on the Soviet State Flag (Pl. LI, 4, and LII to LIV).

The flag of the *Russian Soviet Federative Socialist Republic* is indeed identical with the State Flag except for a broad blue stripe along its hoist.

So broad is the blue stripe which crosses the flag of the *Armenian Soviet Socialist Republic* that it almost forms a tricolour.

In the flag of the *Azerbaijan S.S.R.* the horizontal blue stripe is somewhat narrower and extends along the lower edge.

In that of the *Estonian S.S.R.* the horizontal stripe is a little above the flag's lower edge and is bordered on its own upper edge by a very narrow white stripe, a very narrow blue stripe and a slightly broader white stripe ; these stripes have wavy or " scalloped " margins with the points upwards.

The State emblem on the flag of the *Georgian S.S.R.* is red and appears in a small light blue canton bordered in red and blue ; from the centre of the canton a narrow light blue stripe extends horizontally across the flag.

Along the hoist of the flag of the *White Russian (Byelorussian) S.S.R.* is a red stripe with a curious pattern in white ; this slightly displaces the State Emblem towards the centre of the flag, which is red with a broad light green stripe along its lower edge.

The *Karelo-Finnish S.S.R.*, which in July 1956 reverted to the status of an Autonomous Republic within the R.S.F.S.R., had a narrow green stripe

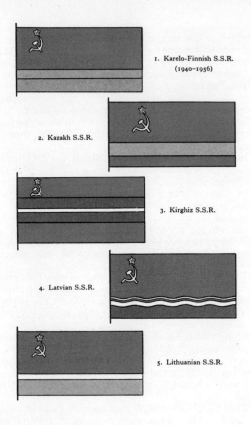

1. Karelo-Finnish S.S.R.
   (1940–1956)

2. Kazakh S.S.R.

3. Kirghiz S.S.R.

4. Latvian S.S.R.

5. Lithuanian S.S.R.

PLATE LIII. THE SOVIET SOCIALIST REPUBLICS—(ii)

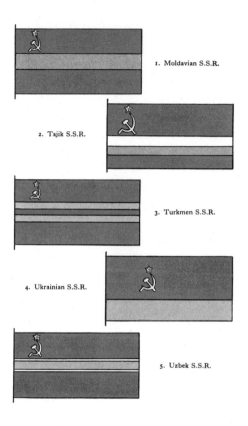

1. Moldavian S.S.R.

2. Tajik S.S.R.

3. Turkmen S.S.R.

4. Ukrainian S.S.R.

5. Uzbek S.S.R.

PLATE LIV. THE SOVIET SOCIALIST REPUBLICS—(iii)

extending along the lower edge of its flag, with a light blue stripe of equal width above it.

The flag of the *Kazakh S.S.R.* is similar, except that its lower stripe is red.

That of the *Kirghiz S.S.R.* would be a red, blue and red tricolour were it not for the narrow white stripe across the centre of the horizontal blue stripe.

Along the lower edge of the flag of the *Latvian S.S.R.* is a blue stripe, and above this are two narrower white stripes separated by a still narrower blue stripe ; the upper edges of all these stripes are wavy.

The lower edge of the flag of the *Lithuanian S.S.R.* is formed by a broad green stripe with a narrower white stripe above it.

The flag of the *Moldavian S.S.R.* is a tricolour of red, green and red, with the green stripe slightly narrower than the others.

The lower half of the flag of the *Tajik S.S.R.* is formed by three stripes, white, green and red ; the green stripe is somewhat narrower than the others.

The flag of the *Turkmen S.S.R.* bears across its centre three narrow stripes, light blue, red and light blue.

On the flag of the *Ukrainian S.S.R.* the State Emblem is placed somewhat lower, and further from the hoist, than on the other flags, and there ia a broad light blue stripe along the lower edge.

Across the centre of the flag of the *Uzbek S.S.R.* is a light blue stripe, bordered by two narrow white stripes.

ASIA

TURKEY.   Though almost the whole of Turkey is
now in Asia, its former capital is in Europe and it was
here that its flag originated.   Because an attempt
by Philip of Macedon to undermine the walls of
Byzantium was disclosed by the moonlight, so it
is said, the city's emblem became the moon, and
so it remained while Byzantium became Constan-
tinople and later Istanbul.   The Turkish Sultan
Othman was centuries later reputed to have seen the
crescent moon in a vision.   For either or both of
these reasons the National Flag and Ensign and
Merchant Flag of Turkey (Pl. LV, 1) displays, on
a red field, the crescent moon and star—the inclusion
of which may be derived from a passage in the
Koran.   The President's Flag, which is square,
adds in the upper hoist a golden flower-like emblem
(Pl. LV, 2).

LEBANON.   The National Flag, Ensign and
Merchant Flag of the Lebanon is a horizontal
tricolour, red, white and red.   On the central
stripe, which is twice as broad as either of the red
stripes, is shown, in green and brown, one of the
Biblical " cedars of Lebanon " (Pl. LV, 3).   The
Jack places in the hoist and fly a broad white stripe
displaying a red anchor, the tricolour thus being
reduced to a square.

TURKEY. 1. National and
Merchant Flag and Ensign

2. President's Flag

3. LEBANON. National and
Merchant Flag and Ensign

4. ISRAEL.
President's Standard

ISRAEL. 5. National Flag

6. Merchant Flag

PLATE LV

142

1. SYRIA. National Flag (until 1958)

2. JORDAN. National Flag

3. IRAQ. National Flag

PLATE LVI

143

ISRAEL. The National Flag of Israel is white, with a blue horizontal stripe near the upper, and another near the lower, edge. In the centre of the flag appears the emblem of the Zionist Movement, the two interlaced equilateral triangles which form the " Shield of David " (Pl. LV, 5). The Ensign and the Merchant Flag are blue, and place the emblem respectively on a white triangle in the hoist and on a white oval near the hoist (Pl. LV, 6).

The President's Standard is square, and displays on a blue field with a white border the Biblical device, in white, of the seven-branched candlestick between two olive-branches ; below is the word " Israel " in Hebrew characters (Pl. LV, 4).

The Israeli Air Force Ensign resembles the National Flag except that it is light blue, and has two horizontal stripes near each of its upper and lower edges, while the national emblem appears within a circle ; all these devices are in dark blue.

THE UNITED ARAB REPUBLIC. Several Mohammedan countries in the Near East show in their flags the colours, black, white, green and red. The National Flag of the United Arab Republic, the state formed from the union of Egypt and Syria in February 1958, is a horizontal tricolour of red, white and black stripes, with two green stars on the white (Pl. LXIII, 1). Though the illustration here appears with African flags, this does not imply precedence of Egypt over Syria in the Republic.

SYRIA. The old National Flag of Syria, now replaced by the flag of the United Arab Republic but illustrated here as a matter of interest (Pl. LVI,

1), was a horizontal tricolour of green, white and black, with three red five-pointed stars on the centre stripe.

JORDAN. In the horizontal tricolour which forms the National Flag of the Hashemite Kingdom of the Jordan the colours are black, white and green, and in the hoist is a red triangle displaying a white seven-pointed star (Pl. LVI, 2). The King's Standard adds a crown, in gold, between the star and the hoist.

IRAQ. The National Flag of Iraq (the region formerly called Mesopotamia) is a vertical tricolour of black, white and green; on the centre of the white stripe is an eight-pointed red star, having at its centre a gold disc bordered with white (Pl. LVI, 3).

SAUDI ARABIA. The National Flag of Saudi Arabia (the Hejaz and Nejd and its Dependencies) is green and displays in Arabic characters, in white, above two crossed swords, the Mohammedan declaration of faith *La illaha illa Allah wa Muhammad Ur-rusul Ullah* (" There is no god but God and Mohammed is the Prophet of God "). The Royal Standard and the Ensign are similar except that the Ensign adds a small white anchor at the top of the fly. The Merchant Flag forms an equilateral triangle and displays the two crossed swords, while the small white anchor appears at the top of the hoist. (Pl. LVII, 1, 2).

YEMEN. The flags of the Moutawakilite Kingdom

SAUDI ARABIA. 1. National Flag   2. Merchant Flag

3. YEMEN. National Flag

PLATE LVII

of Yemen are red. The National Flag displays in white a traditional Arabic emblem, the scimitar, and five stars, said to represent both the five divisions of the country and the five dogmas of the Mohammedan faith (Pl. LVII, 3). The Royal Standard bears an inscription in white Arabic characters.

THE TRUCIAL COAST. The Trucial Coast, or Pirate Coast, which is under British protection,

1. PERSIA. National and Merchant Flag

PERSIA.   2. Jack

3. Shah's Standard

4. AFGHANISTAN. National Flag

PLATE LVIII

147

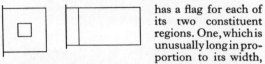

has a flag for each of its two constituent regions. One, which is unusually long in proportion to its width, is red except for a broad white stripe in the hoist. The other is a white square, and bears a small red square at its centre.

OMAN, MUSCAT AND THE INDEPENDENT TRIBES. The flag of Oman, Muscat and the Independent Tribes is red.

KUWAIT. The National Flag of the State of *Kuwait* consists of a horizontal tricolour, green over white over red, with a black inset at the hoist.

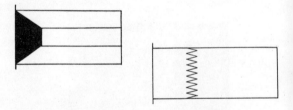

BAHREIN. The State or Island Flag of Bahrein is red, with a broad white stripe along the hoist; the edge of the stripe may be either straight or deeply serrated. On the Sheikh's Personal Standard the white stripe, whose edge is serrated, extends to form narrower stripes along the flag's upper and lower edges.

QATAR. The National Flag of Qatar is maroon, with a broad white stripe along the hoist. The stripe is serrated.

PERSIA. The National and Merchant Flag of Persia (Iran) is a horizontal tricolour, green, white and red (Pl. LVIII, 1), unusually long in proportion to its breadth; its colours were at one time as unusual as its shape, apple-green, white and pink. The Ensign and Army Flag display at their centre the National Emblem, a lion grasping a scimitar with the sun rising behind, surrounded by a wreath and with a crown above; the Government Flag displays the armed lion without crown or wreath.

The Standard of the Shah displays the crown at the centre of a square light-blue flag; a very small canton displays the National Emblem on a field of the national tricolour (Pl. LVIII, 3).

The Jack is square and displays the emblem on a green field (Pl. LVIII, 2).

AFGHANISTAN. The National Flag of Afghanistan is a vertical tricolour of black, red and green; the other traditional Moslem colour, white, is used to display the emblem of a mosque with an open door, flanked on each side by a flag and within a wreath tied by a ribbon bearing the name "Afghanistan" in Arabic characters (Pl. LVIII, 4).

The obverse of the Royal Standard displays a similar emblem in white on a red field; the reverse shows an Arabic inscription within the wreath.

149

1. BURMA. President's Flag

2. BURMA. National Flag

3. THAILAND. Royal Standard

THAILAND. 4. National
and Merchant Flag

5. Ensign

PLATE LIX

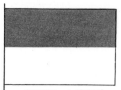

INDONESIA. 1. National
and Merchant Flag

2. President's Flag

3. INDONESIA. Jack

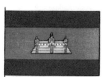

4. CAMBODIA. National Flag

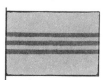

5. VIET-NAM. National Flag

6. LAOS. National Flag

7. PHILIPPINES. National and Merchant Flag and Ensign

PLATE LX

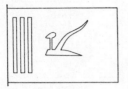

JAMMU AND KASH-
MIR. The red flag of
Jammu and Kashmir dis-
plays, in white, a sil-
houette of a native plough;
in the hoist are three
vertical bars.

BURMA. The National Flag of the Republic of
Burma is red; the blue canton displays a large
five-pointed star surrounded by five smaller stars
in white; the large star commemorates the Anti-
Fascist resistance movement in the Second World
War, the others represent the unity of Burma's
five races (Pl. LIX, 2). The Ensign uses the same
canton in a flag which otherwise resembles the
British White Ensign.

The President's Flag displays, on a field of
orange-red, the traditional emblem of Burma, a
peacock "in his pride" (with tail outspread)
(Pl. LIX, 1).

THAILAND. Although Thailand (Siam) is
traditionally the "land of the sacred white elephant"
this emblem does not appear on the National and
Merchant Flag, which is striped horizontally, red,
white, blue (of double width), white and red
(Pl. LIX, 4). It does however appear on the Ensign,
upon a red circle at the flag's centre (Pl. LIX, 5).

The Royal Standard is yellow and bears a representation, in red, of the "Garuda", a sacred bird
of the Brahman mythology (Pl. LIX, 3).

INDO-CHINA. Each of the three Associated
States of Indo-China has its own flag. That of

Cambodia is a horizontal tricolour, blue, red and blue ; on the red stripe, which is broader than the others, appears, in white, a conventionalised pagoda (Pl. LX, 4). That of *Laos* is red and displays the national emblem, a three-headed elephant, in white, beneath a parasol (Pl. LX, 6). That of *Viet-nam* is yellow or orange and is crossed horizontally at its centre by three narrow red stripes (Pl. LX, 5); but the flag of the *Viet-Minh Communists* is red and bears a large yellow five-pointed star in the centre.

INDONESIA. The National Flag and Merchant Flag of the Republic of the United States of Indonesia is divided horizontally, red above white (Pl. LX, 1). On its obverse the Ensign displays an anchor within a wreath on a royal blue field, the Army Flag a symbolical eagle below a star and within a wreath on a field of emerald green, and the Air Force Ensign an emblem including a soaring bird on a sky-blue field ; all these devices are golden-yellow. The reverse of all three flags shows the Indonesian Coat-of-Arms. The Jack bears nine horizontal stripes, alternately red and white (Pl. LX, 3).

The President's Flag is canary-yellow, and depicts in golden-yellow a large five-pointed star within a wreath of rice and cotton blades (Pl. LX, 2).

THE PHILIPPINES. The National Flag and Ensign and Merchant Flag of the Philippines is divided horizontally, blue above red ; in the hoist is a white equilateral triangle with a golden eight-rayed sun emblem in the centre and a golden star in each of the angles (Pl. LX, 7). The Jack places similar emblems on a blue field.

1. NATIONALIST CHINA. National Flag and Ensign

2. CHINESE PEOPLE'S REPUBLIC. National and Merchant Flag

3. NEPAL

4. TIBET

PLATE LXI

JAPAN. 1. Emperor's Standard   2. National and Merchant Flag and Jack

3. JAPAN. Ensign   4. SOUTH KOREA. National Flag

5. NORTH KOREA. National Flag

PLATE LXII

155

The President's Flag is sky-blue and bears the sun emblem on a circle of fifty-two stars; superimposed upon the emblem is a red triangle with a gold star in each of its angles and a sea-lion grasping a dagger.

NATIONALIST CHINA. The National Flag and Ensign of Nationalist China is red ; the canton—which in itself forms the Jack—is blue and displays in white a conventionalised sun emblem emitting twelve rays (Pl. LXI, 1). The Merchant Flag places four wavy golden stripes horizontally across the field.

THE PEOPLE'S REPUBLIC OF CHINA. The National Flag and Merchant Flag of the People's Republic of China is red and depicts in the upper hoist a gold five-pointed star and four smaller stars arranged in an arc (Pl. LXI, 2). The smaller stars are said to represent the four social classes of the Republic—workers, peasants, petty bourgeoisie and "patriotic capitalists"—and the larger star the "common programme" in which they unite.

NEPAL. The double flag of Nepal—which, it will be remembered, was among those unfurled by Hillary and Tensing on Mount Everest—consists of two blue-bordered red right-angled triangles, one above the other. On the upper triangle appears a stylised emblem of the crescent moon, on the lower a stylised emblem of the sun (Pl. LXI, 3).

TIBET. The flag of Tibet represents a snowy mountain behind which the rising sun is emitting red rays across a blue sky ; superimposed on the mountain two lions are shown fighting for a pearl and above them is a jewel emblem (Pl. LXI, 4).

SIKKIM. The flag of Sikkim is white, but except along the fly it is bordered red, white and blue, the red forming the flag's edge. At the centre of the field appears a wheel-like emblem in red, and around it are several other symbols in red, blue, green and yellow.

BHUTAN. The flag of Bhutan is halved diagonally orange-yellow and red and displays an heraldic wingless dragon in white.

MONGOLIA. The flag of the Mongolian People's

Republic is a vertical tricolour, red, blue and red; on the red stripe at the hoist appears a group of symbols of magical significance surmounted by a star, all in gold.

JAPAN. The " Land of the Rising Sun ", Japan places a suitable emblem on most of its flags. On the National Flag, Merchant Flag and Jack, the sun appears as a red disc at the centre of a white field (Pl. LXII, 2). On the Ensign, which is worn by units of the Coastal Defence Force, it is displaced somewhat towards the hoist and is shown emitting sixteen red rays across the white field (Pl. LXII, 3).

The Emperor's Standard (Pl. LXII, 1) displays another of Japan's national emblems, the chrysanthemum, gold on a red field.

SOUTH KOREA. The present flag of South Korea is a variant of the former Korean flag. The National Flag is white and bears at its centre an ancient mystical emblem, a circle halved by a curved dividing line : the two halves, red above blue, are called the *Yang* and the *Yin*, representing the two complementary powers of nature ; patterns of black lines, called "trigrams", towards the flag's corners, also have a magical significance (Pl. LXII, 4). The Ensign and Jack worn by naval vessels are blue ; in the canton the divided circle is superimposed upon two black anchors.

NORTH KOREA. The National Flag of North Korea, the Democratic Korean People's Republic, is a tricolour in which two horizontal blue stripes are separated from a broader red stripe by a white fimbriation ; near the hoist the red stripe displays a red star on a white circle (Pl. LXII, 5).

1. UNITED ARAB REPUBLIC. National Flag

2. EGYPT. National Flag (until 1958)

3. SUDAN. National Flag

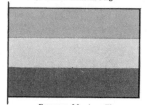

4. ETHIOPIA. Merchant Flag

PLATE LXIII

AFRICA

EGYPT. The Mohammedan colours, green and white, and the Mohammedan emblem, the crescent moon, appeared on the former National and Merchant Flag of Egypt, illustrated here (Pl. LXIII, 2), although since the formation of the United Arab Republic in February 1958 (see page 144), it is no longer in use.

THE SUDAN. The National Flag of the Sudan is a horizontal tricolour, blue, gold and green (Pl. LXIII, 3). The colours symbolise respectively the River Nile, the desert, and the fertility brought by the river.

ETHIOPIA. The Merchant Flag of Ethiopia (Abyssinia) is a horizontal tricolour, green, gold and red (Pl. LXIII, 4). The National Flag may depict on the central stripe, in green, the National Emblem, a Crowned Lion bearing a cross.

ERITREA. Eritrea used the flag of Ethiopia.

LIBERIA. Founded about 1821 by the American Colonisation Society as a refuge for freed slaves, Liberia naturally compliments the U.S.A. in the design of its flags. The National Flag, Ensign and Merchant Flag bears eleven horizontal red and white stripes; a small canton displays one five-pointed star on a blue field (Pl. LXIV, 1). The Jack is similar to the flag's canton.

CONGO. The *Independent Republic of Congo* (Pl. LXIV, 2) has a bright blue flag with a five-pointed star in the centre. Six small yellow five-pointed stars are spaced in a vertical line at the hoist.

LIBYA. The Mohammedan colours and emblem appear on the flags of Libya. The National Flag is a horizontal tricolour, red, black and green; on the central stripe, which is double the width of either of the others, appear, in white, the crescent moon and star (Pl. LXIV, 3).

MOROCCO. The National and Merchant Flag of Morocco is red, and bears, outlined in green, the ancient magical device of the Pentagram, a variant of Solomon's Seal (Pl. LXIV, 4).

TUNISIA. The National and Merchant Flag of Tunisia is also red; at its centre is a white circle bearing, in red, the Mohammedan device of the crescent moon and five-pointed star (Pl. LXV, 2).

ALGERIA. The Algerian flag is vertically divided, half green and half white, the green being in the hoist. In the centre is a red crescent containing a red star (Pl. LXV,1).

THE REPUBLIC OF SOUTH AFRICA

Unique in design, the National Flag of the Republic of South Africa, which is also the Merchant Flag

1. LIBERIA. National and Merchant Flag and Ensign

2. CONGO. National Flag

3. LIBYA. National Flag

4. MOROCCO. National and Merchant Flag

PLATE LXIV

1. ALGERIA. National Flag

2. TUNISIA. National Flag

3. National Flag of Republic of South Africa

4. Ensign of S.A. Naval Forces

PLATE LXV.

and the Jack, indicates the countries by whose peoples the region was developed. It is a horizontal tricolour of orange, white and blue, similar to the historic *Prinsevlag* of William of Orange. In the centre of the white stripe the former flag of the Orange Free State is shown hanging vertically. Towards the hoist the British Union Flag is shown spread horizontally. Towards the fly, also spread horizontally, is the former Transvaal *Vierkleur*, the Netherlands tricolour with a broad green stripe along the hoist (Pl. LXV, 3).

The Ensign of the South African Naval Forces places the National Flag in the canton of a white flag bearing a dark green cross of St. George type (Pl. LXV, 4).

DAHOMEY. The flag consists of a vertical emerald green stripe at the hoist with horizontal stripes, yellow over red, in the fly (Pl. LXVI, 1).

NIGER. *Niger* uses three horizontal stripes of equal width, orange over white over emerald green, with a disc in orange in the middle (Pl. LXVI, 2).

MAURITANIA. The *Islamic Republic of Mauritania* adopted an emerald green flag, bearing a crescent and five-pointed star, in gold, in the centre (Pl. LXVI, 3).

FRENCH CONGO. The flag of *French Congo* comprises a broad diagonal stripe in yellow, between two triangles, emerald green (at the hoist) and red (Pl. LXVI, 4).

164

MADAGASCAR. *Madagascar* uses a flag divided horizontally, red over emerald green, with a wide vertical white stripe at the hoist (Pl. LXVI, 5).

MALI. The flag is a vertical tricolour, emerald green (at the hoist), yellow and red; the middle stripe bears a symbolic representation of a Negro dancer with arms uplifted (Pl. LXVI, 6).

CENTRAL AFRICAN REPUBLIC. This flag consists of four horizontal stripes of equal width, blue (at the top), white, emerald green, and yellow; overall a red vertical stripe in the centre. A five-pointed yellow star is positioned at the hoist on the blue stripe (Pl. LXVI, 7).

GABOON. *Gaboon* adopted a flag comprising three horizontal stripes of equal width, green (top), golden yellow, and royal blue (Pl. LXVI, 8).

TOGO. The flag has five horizontal stripes of equal width, three emerald green and two yellow. A white five-pointed star appears on a large red canton in the upper hoist (Pl. LXVII, 1).

CHAD. *Chad* has a vertical tricolour, blue (at the hoist), yellow, and red (Pl. LXVII, 2).

CAMEROON REPUBLIC. The flag is a vertical tricolour, emerald green (at the hoist), red, and yellow. These colours are said to represent respectively the luxuriant vegetation of the south, sovereignty or authority, and the sun in the extreme north. In the upper portion of the green stripe appear two five-pointed yellow stars (Pl. LXVII, 3).

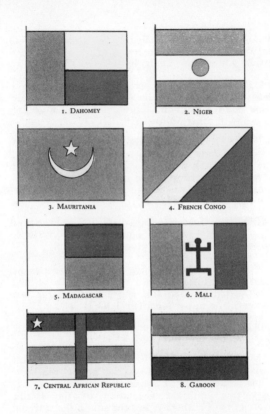

1. DAHOMEY   2. NIGER

3. MAURITANIA   4. FRENCH CONGO

5. MADAGASCAR   6. MALI

7. CENTRAL AFRICAN REPUBLIC   8. GABOON

PLATE LXVI. AFRICAN STATES: NATIONAL FLAGS

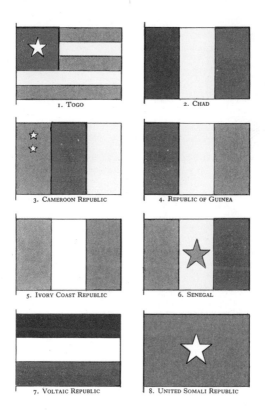

1. TOGO   2. CHAD

3. CAMEROON REPUBLIC   4. REPUBLIC OF GUINEA

5. IVORY COAST REPUBLIC   6. SENEGAL

7. VOLTAIC REPUBLIC   8. UNITED SOMALI REPUBLIC

PLATE LXVII. AFRICAN STATES: NATIONAL FLAGS

REPUBLIC OF GUINEA. This has a flag consisting of three vertical stripes of equal width, red (at the hoist), yellow, and emerald green (Pl. LXVII, 4).

IVORY COAST REPUBLIC. A vertical tricolour is used, orange (at the hoist), white, and emerald green (Pl. LXVII, 5).

SENEGAL. The flag is a vertical tricolour, green (at the hoist), gold, and red, with a five-pointed green star on the centre stripe (Pl. LXVII, 6).

VOLTAIC REPUBLIC. The *Voltaic Republic* adopted a horizontal tricolour, black over white over red (Pl. LXVII, 7).

UNITED SOMALI REPUBLIC. The former British Somaliland, together with Italian Somalia, is now the United Somali Republic and uses a light blue flag bearing a large white five-pointed star in the centre (Pl. LXVII, 8).

THE AMERICAS

THE PAN-AMERICAN UNION

Formed in 1890 to promote commercial and diplomatic relations and general co-operation between the American Republics—including the U.S.A.—the Pan-American Union, formerly known as the Organisation of American States, has its own flag. This is white and bears three reddish-purple crosses, said to represent the three ships of Columbus ; behind the central cross, which is slightly larger than the others, appears an ancient symbol of the Incas, the rising sun, in bronze (Pl. LXVIII, 1).

LATIN AMERICA

The Union is not without a precedent: in 1494, shortly after " the Americas " were discovered, the Pope decreed that they should be divided between Spain and Portugal. Ignored by the Protestant nations, this ruling was ineffective in much of North America but decided the future of the rest of the New World, the greater part of which was long subject to Spain. Only when the Spanish dynasty was overthrown by Napoleon did the region disintegrate into a number of independent— and often warring—republics. In token of their revolutionary origin, many of them adopted tricolour flags.

MEXICO. Spanish rule even extended into North America, where what was then called " New Spain " is now Mexico. Its Merchant Flag is a vertical tricolour, green, white and red (Pl. LXVIII, 2). The National Flag, Ensign and President's Standard display on the central stripe the National Emblem, an eagle perched on a prickly pear plant and

holding a snake in its beak: this device refers to an Aztec legend. The square Jack is striped diagonally, white, green and red; on each stripe is a gold circle with a wavy edge, and the central stripe also depicts a white anchor (Pl. LXVIII, 3).

THE CARIBBEAN ISLANDS (ANTILLES)

CUBA. The National Flag, Ensign and Merchant Flag of Cuba is the historic " Lone Star Banner " under which the island won freedom from Spanish rule in 1898. It consists of five horizontal blue and white stripes; in the hoist the " Lone Star ", in white, appears on a red equilateral triangle (Pl. LXIX, 1). The Jack, another of Cuba's historic flags, displays the star on a red canton; the rest of the flag's upper half is white and the whole of its lower half blue (Pl. LXIX, 2).

DOMINICA. The greater part of the island known as Hispaniola or San Domingo is formed by the Dominican Republic. On its Merchant Flag is a white cross of St. George type quartering the field

1. The Pan-American Union

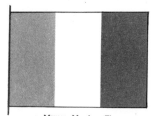

2. Mexico. Merchant Flag

3. Mexico. Jack

PLATE LXVIII

blue and red (Pl. LXIX, 3). The National Flag and Ensign place at the centre of the cross the national Coat-of-Arms. The President's Flag places the Ensign in the canton of a white flag with a gold anchor in its fly.

HAITI. The Merchant Flag of Haiti is halved horizontally, blue over red (Pl. LXIX, 4). It may be derived from the French tricolour—the white stripe representing the white men having been removed, the colours may symbolise respectively the negroes and the mulattoes. The National Flag and Ensign bear at the centre a white rectangle displaying six national flags, two pendants, two

cannon with two piles of round-shot, two an-chors, six rifles and a drum, grouped round a palm tree surmounted by the Cap of Liberty, and a scroll bears the motto *L'Union fait la Force* (" Union makes Strength ").

CENTRAL AMERICA

Having gained their freedom from rule by Spain, the Spanish possessions south of Mexico for a time remained united as the *Federation of Central American States*, whose flag was a horizontal tricolour, blue, white and blue. Though in 1839 they separated, the countries formerly in the Federation still use this emblem, varying it however to show their present independence.

GUATEMALA. Guatemala has transformed the Federation's flag into a *vertical* tricolour, blue, white and blue (Pl. LXX, 1). This in itself forms the Merchant Flag; the National Flag and Ensign

displays on the central stripe the national Emblem: two crossed rifles and swords surmounted by a scroll bearing the date on which the country obtained its freedom, within a laurel wreath tied by a ribbon of the national colours and surmounted by a Central American bird, the *quetzal*.

HONDURAS. Three of the other countries formerly in the Federation retain the horizontal tricolour of blue, white and blue, but distinguish it by emblems on the central stripe. The National and Merchant Flag of Honduras places on the stripe five blue five-pointed stars arranged saltire-fashion (Pl. LXX, 2). The Ensign displays a badge showing a

pyramidal structure rising from a sea symbolising the Atlantic and Pacific Oceans; an oval bears the words *Libre, Soberana, e Independiente* (" Free, Sovereign and Independent "); it is flanked by two cornucopias and below is a landscape and the tools of industry.

1. CUBA. National and Merchant Flag and Ensign

2. CUBA. Jack

3. DOMINICAN REPUBLIC. Merchant Flag

4. HAITI. Merchant Flag

PLATE LXIX

174

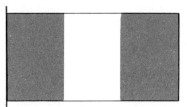

1. GUATEMALA. Merchant Flag

2. HONDURAS. National and Merchant Flag

3. EL SALVADOR. Merchant Flag

PLATE LXX

EL SALVADOR. The Merchant Flag of El Salvador distinguishes the blue, white and blue horizontal tricolour by placing on the central stripe the words *Dios, Union y Libertad* (" God, Union and Freedom ") (Pl. LXX, 3). The National Flag

and Ensign similarly place the national Badge: a triangle superimposed on five National Flags and displaying five mountains rising out of the sea—the five volcanoes of Central America—with a staff at their centre bearing a Cap of Liberty emitting beams of light; around is a laurel wreath.

NICARAGUA. On all the flags of Nicaragua, the National Flag, Ensign and Merchant Flag, appear the country's badge, a triangle showing the five mountains, the sea, and the Cap of Liberty, with the sun rising over the horizon and a rainbow overhead. The flag itself is a horizontal tricolour, blue, white and blue (Pl. LXXI, 1).

COSTA RICA. Costa Rica has transformed its emblem from a tricolour into a flag striped horizontally, dark blue, white, red, white and dark blue; this in itself forms the National and Merchant Flag (Pl. LXXI, 2). On the central stripe, which is twice as wide as any of the others, the Ensign and Government Flag places a white circle bearing the National Badge: an ornate shield displaying three mountains (representing volcanoes) between the two oceans, on each of which is a sailing ship; above are five white stars.

PANAMA. Panama, which became independent much later than the other Central American States, has a very distinctive flag. The National Flag, Ensign, and Merchant Flag is quartered: white with a blue five-pointed star, red, blue, and white with a red five-pointed star (Pl. LXXI, 3). These colours, and the star ·emblem, may have been adopted in compliment to the United States, which controls the Panama Canal Zone.

SOUTH AMERICA

The northern part of South America was formerly united as *Great Colombia*. Though now separated to form three independent republics, these recall their earlier association in the colour of their flags, all based on the tricolour which showed their revolt against Spanish rule.

COLOMBIA. The National Flag and Jack of Colombia is a horizontal tricolour, yellow (of double width), dark blue and red. The Merchant Flag places at its centre a red-bordered blue oval con-

1. NICARAGUA. National and Merchant Flag and Ensign

2. COSTA RICA. National and Merchant Flag

3. PANAMA. National and Merchant Flag and Ensign

PLATE LXXI
178

taining a white eight-pointed star (Pl. LXXII, 1). The Ensign similarly places a red circle containing a white disc displaying the National Arms: a shield displays a pomegranate between two cornucopias above a seascape which shows the two oceans on each of which is a sailing-ship, and which is dominated by the Cap of Liberty; it is flanked on each side by two National Flags; the crest is a condor and a scroll bears the words *Libertad y Orden* (" Liberty and Order ").

VENEZUELA. On the horizontal tricolour of yellow, blue and red which forms the flags of Venezuela the stripes are equal in width. The Merchant Flag places on the central stripe seven white five-pointed stars in a semi-circle (Pl. LXXII, 2). The National Flag and Ensign add the national arms in the upper hoist: a shield displays a sheaf of corn, a device of flags and swords, and an untamed wild horse; it is flanked by wreaths of palm and sco laurel; two cornucopias form the crest and below is an elaborate scroll commemorating events significant in the country's history.

179

ECUADOR. The tricolour of Ecuador is similar to that of Colombia. The Merchant Flag is the plain tricolour of yellow (of double width), light blue and red (Pl. LXXII, 3). The National Flag, Ensign, Jack and President's Standard place the Coat-of-Arms at the centre: an oval shield depicts a snow-topped mountain, Chimborazo, and a steamer out at sea, above is a sun emblem and four zodiacal signs; it is flanked on each side by two National Flags; below is the fasces and the crest is a condor.

PERU. The tricolour which forms the Merchant Flag of Peru is vertical, red, white and red (Pl. LXXIII, 1). The National Flag and Ensign place the National Arms on the white stripe: a shield displays a llama, a cinchona tree and a cornucopia; it is superimposed on two pairs of crossed National Flags, and a wreath forms the crest. The Jack places these Arms at the centre of a white red-bordered square.

CHILE. The canton of the National Flag, Ensign and Merchant Flag of Chile is blue and displays a white five-pointed star; the remainder of the flag's upper half is white and its lower half is red (Pl. LXXIII, 2). The Jack is blue, with a small white star at its centre.

The President's Flag places the National Coat-of-Arms at the centre of  the National Flag: the white star appears on a shield divided horizontally blue above red; the supporters are a *huemal* (Chilean deer) and a condor, the crest is formed by three rhea's feathers, blue, white and red, and a scroll bears the motto *Por la Razon o la Fuerza* (" By Right and Might ").

ARGENTINA. The Merchant Flag of the Argentine Republic is a horizontal tricolour, light blue, white and light blue. The National Flag, Ensign and Government Flag add a stylised sun emblem in the centre of the white stripe (Pl. LXXIII, 3). This emblem on a white blue-bordered field forms the Jack. The President's Flag is light blue with a white star at each corner, and displays the National Arms: on an oval field, blue above white, two clasped hands support a staff topped by the Cap of Liberty; it is surrounded by a laurel wreath which partly obscures the sun emblem above.

181

1. COLOMBIA. Merchant Flag

2. VENEZUELA. Merchant Flag

3. ECUADOR. Merchant Flag

PLATE LXXII

182

1. PERU. Merchant Flag

2. CHILE. National and Merchant Flag and Ensign

3. ARGENTINA. National and Government Flag and Ensign

PLATE LXXIII.

183

URUGUAY. Though the flags of Uruguay are strikingly unlike those of the other South American countries they recall the nation's former association with Argentina by using a conventionalised sun emblem. This appears in gold on a small white canton on the National Flag, Ensign and Merchant Flag; the fly consists of nine white and blue stripes (Pl. LXXII, 1). The Jack also suggests association with Argentina in being a horizontal tricolour, blue, white and blue, but it is crossed by a red diagonal stripe (Pl. LXXIV, 2).

The President's Flag is white and displays at its centre the National Arms. They consist of an oval

shield quartered blue and white and depicting a pair of scales, a fortress-crowned hill, a horse, and a golden bull, the symbols respectively of justice, power, freedom, and wealth; the shield is surrounded by a wreath of olive and laurel and the sun emblem is shown rising above its upper edge.

PARAGUAY. The National Flag, Ensign and Merchant Flag of Paraguay is a horizontal tricolour of red, white and blue; at the centre of the white stripe the obverse places a circle displaying a gold five-sided star within a wreath of palm and olive (Pl. LXXIV, 4); the reverse places the device of a lion guarding the Cap of Liberty. The Jack is a saltire formed of a blue stripe and a red stripe, with a gold star on a white circle as its centre (Pl. LXXIV, 3).

The President's Flag is blue with a gold star in each corner; at its centre another gold star is depicted within a wreath upon a white disc with a border of blue, white and red.

BOLIVIA. The Merchant Flag and Private Citizen's Flag of Bolivia is a red, gold and green tricolour (Pl. LXXV, 1). The National Flag and the President's Flag place on the central stripe the Coat-of-Arms: an oval shield displays a landscape including the mineral-rich mountain of Potosim,

 a breadfruit tree, and a llama, symbolising the country's natural resources; on the border, which is half yellow and half blue, appear nine golden stars; the shield is superimposed on a trophy of flags and weapons and above it a condor is shown alighting on a wreath.

1. URUGUAY. National and Merchant Flag and Ensign

2. URUGUAY. Jack

3. PARAGUAY. Jack

4. PARAGUAY. National and Merchant Flag and Ensign

PLATE LXXIV.

186

1. BOLIVIA. Merchant Flag

2. BRAZIL. National and
Merchant Flag and Ensign

3. BRAZIL. Jack

PLATE LXXV.
187

BRAZIL. The contrast between the flags of Brazil and those of the other Latin American countries has a historical basis. Whereas those countries were colonised from Spain, Brazil was colonised from Portugal, whose influence is shown in its emblems; they retain the yellow diamond on a green field which they bore in the region's colonial days, but the former Imperial emblem on the diamond (an armillary sphere similar to that on the Portuguese flag) has been replaced by another astronomical emblem: a blue celestial globe sprinkled with stars and girdled with a white equator bearing the words *Ordem e Progresso* (" Order and Progress "). This forms the National Flag, Ensign and Merchant Flag (Pl. LXXV, 2). The Jack is blue and bears a cross formed of white stars (Pl. LXXV, 3).

The President's Flag is green and bears the National Arms: on a large five-pointed star whose arms are green and gold with a red and white edging, within a wreath of coffee and tobacco, appear the five stars of the Southern Cross, white on a blue field, within a circle of twenty stars representing the states of the Brazilian Federation.

MISCELLANEOUS FLAGS

HOUSE FLAGS OF SHIPPING COMPANIES

The custom for merchant ships to wear special flags denoting their ownership is of long standing. To show the patronage of Queen Elizabeth I the *Levant* or *Muscovy Company* displayed the St. George's Cross, duly fimbriated in white, superimposed upon the contemporary Royal Standard; and, as already stated, the Stars and Stripes may have been evolved from the *East India Company's* Ensign (Pl. XXIII, 2, p. 73).

The modern House Flags started coming into use during the Mechanical Revolution; to distinguish steamships from sailing-vessels some firms placed above their House Flag a special " Steam Cornet ", which is still occasionally used, as by the *Glen Line* (Pl. LXXVI, 3). By long tradition, House Flags are normally worn at the main; an exception is that of the *Brocklebank Line* (Pl. LXXVI, 5), which is worn at the fore.

As will be seen, House Flags are varied, and some are attractive ; a few are of special interest because of their origin or significance. When two firms combine, they may either use both their flags, as does the *Cunard White Star Line* (Pl. LXXVI, 1), or merge them to form a new emblem : in the *Union Castle Line* House Flag the St. Andrew's Saltire comes from the former Castle Line, as does

1. Cunard White Star Line

2. Union Castle Line   3. Glen Line   4. Clan Line

5. Brocklebank Line   6. Shell tanker fleet

7. British Railways   8. General Steam Navigation Co

PLATE LXXVI. HOUSE FLAGS OF SHIPPING
COMPANIES

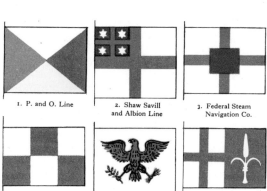

1. P. and O. Line

2. Shaw Savill
and Albion Line

3. Federal Steam
Navigation Co.

4. Canadian Pacific Lines

5. United States Line

6. Italia Line

7. Cammell Laird & Co.

8. Vickers Armstrongs Ltd.

9. John Brown & Co. Ltd.

10. Harland & Wolff Ltd.

PLATE LXXVII. HOUSE FLAGS OF SHIPPING AND
SHIPBUILDING COMPANIES

the white diamond at the centre, the St. Patrick's Saltire from the former Union Line (Pl. LXXVI, 2).

As might be expected, a favourite emblem for Scottish Lines is the Rampant Lion of Scotland, but without the Tressure which would convert it into a royal emblem. It is used, for example, by the *Clan Line*, whose ships also wear Jacks displaying the respective tartans after which they are named (Pl. LXXVI, 4).

Some House Flags are familiar both at sea and on land; among them is the " Shell " emblem of the Shell tanker fleet (Pl. LXXVI, 6). The emblem adopted by the *British Railways*, the lion astride a wheel, so conspicuously displayed inland, figures at the centre of a saltire of unusual design on the House Flags of the organisation's ships (Pl. LXXVI, 7). Another flag well known in British coastal waters is that of the *General Steam Navigation Co.*, with the terrestrial globe which indicates that Company's intention to operate its ships much more widely afield (Pl. LXXVI, 8).

Unheraldic though distinctive, the " envelope " flag of the *Peninsular and Oriental Line* (Pl. LXXVII, 1) is historic, not to say romantic, in origin. In token of assistance rendered during periods of political unrest to the Queens of both countries in the Iberian Peninsula, the flag combines their royal colours, the white and blue of Portugal with the red and gold of Spain. Another House Flag of historical significance is that of the *Shaw Savill and Albion Line* (Pl. LXXVII, 2), similar to the former flag of New Zealand.

No House Flag may resemble any national or official flag, and among the emblems thus proscribed is the Command Flag of an Admiral of the Royal Navy, the St. George's Cross. A ship's master whose vessel once sported this was peremptorily ordered to strike it. Forced to comply, he triumphantly re-hoisted it with a blue rectangle sewn at its centre—and this is now the House Flag of the *Federal Steam Navigation Co.* (Pl. LXXVII, 3).

The chequered flag of the *Canadian Pacific Line* is based on the method used on the early maps showing the route of the Canadian Pacific Railway to indicate that alternate tracts of land should belong to the Government and to the Company (Pl. LXXVII, 4).

The House Flags of other countries are as varied as those of Britain. Some make use of an appropriate national emblem, like the Eagle displayed on the flag of the *United States Line* (Pl. LXXVII, 5). The flag of the *Italia Line* combines the red cross of Genoa with the halberd, white on red, of Trieste (Pl. LXXVII, 6).

HOUSE FLAGS OF SHIPBUILDING COMPANIES

Many shipbuilding companies also have their own House Flags. Such a flag is displayed, along with that of the prospective owners, while a vessel is being launched. Four of these Shipbuilding House Flags are illustrated (Pl. LXXVII, 7–10); that of *Cammell Laird and Co.* is an amusing example of punning heraldry.

YACHT FLAGS

Pleasure yachting has an elaborate etiquette of flag usage. Like other vessels, yachts must display

N

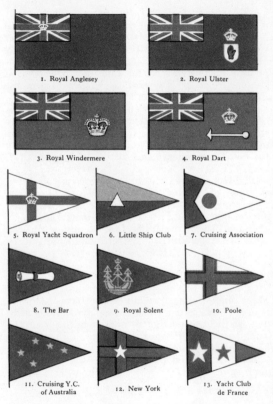

1. Royal Anglesey   2. Royal Ulster

3. Royal Windermere   4. Royal Dart

5. Royal Yacht Squadron   6. Little Ship Club   7. Cruising Association

8. The Bar   9. Royal Solent   10. Poole

11. Cruising Y.C. of Australia   12. New York   13. Yacht Club de France

PLATE LXXVIII. YACHT CLUBS

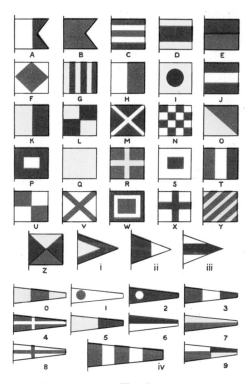

PLATE LXXIX THE INTERNATIONAL
CODE OF SIGNALS

near the stern a national emblem; for British clubs this is one of the Ensigns. The Royal Yacht Squadron alone shares with the Royal Navy the privilege of wearing the White Ensign (Pl. VI, 1, p. 31); other clubs use, in descending order of seniority, the Blue Ensign undefaced, the Blue Ensign defaced with a special badge; the Red Ensign similarly defaced; and the Red Ensign (Pl. IX, 1, p. 39). Each yacht or sailing club, moreover, has its own *burgee*—for British clubs a triangular flag—worn at the mainmast head or, in mastless power-driven boats, from a staff over or near the wheelhouse.

Pl. LXXVIII illustrates various methods of defacing the Blue or Red Ensign, as well as the burgees of certain well-known yacht clubs.

THE INTERNATIONAL CODE OF SIGNALS

Though fighting ships have long had methods of conveying orders or information to one another, only in comparatively recent times have flag signals been codified. The first commercial code was drawn up in 1817 by Captain Marryat, and this formed the basis for what has now become the *International Code of Signals*. It provides a flag for each letter of the alphabet, a pennant for each of the ten digits, three triangular " substitutes " to avoid the need for duplicating the other flags (i-iii), and the " Code and Answering Pennant " (iv). (Pl. LXXIX).

These flags enable an incredible variety of signals to be given, being displayed singly or in hoists of from two to five; the fewer their number the more urgent is the signal. The two swallow-tailed flags act as warnings, **A** that a vessel is undergoing a speed trial and **B** that she is taking in or discharging explosives. Flag **D** is also a warning that a ship is manoeuvring with difficulty. K warns another vessel that she should " stop instantly " and **U** that she is " standing into danger ". **O** conveys the grim message " man overboard!" Other flags request help, **F** because a ship is disabled, **V** because she requires assistance, and **W** because she requires *medical* assistance.

Two flags are frequently seen in harbours, **Q** which means that a vessel declares herself healthy and requests practique (permission to enter port), and **H** (or a similar flag divided horizontally, white over red) that she carries a pilot. Probably the most widely-known of all such flags is the famous " Blue Peter ", the **P** which announces that a vessel is about to sail.

Two-flag hoists also include signals of distress or warning as well as messages concerning the handling of ships—thus **SC** enquires a vessel's name and **RX** makes the dramatic announcement " Mutiny! " Three-flag hoists are more general, **PYU** conveying the cheery greeting " Good voyage! " Four-flag signals comprise geographical localities and the names of ships, **AGJV** signifying " Glasgow " and **GBTT** the " Queen Mary ". The Answering Pennant is used for such purposes as to show that a message has been understood.

HOUSE FLAGS OF AIR LINES

Most of the leading Air Lines have their House Flags, flown over airfields and elsewhere. Well known in Britain are the " Speedbird ", gold on

1. B.O.A.C.

2. B.E.A.

3. Cambrian Air Services

4. Scottish Air Lines

5. Qantas

6. S. African Airways

7. Australian
National Airways

8. Trans-Canada Airlines

9. Pakistan International
Airlines

PLATE LXXX COMMONWEALTH AIR LINES

1. Pan American World Airways

2. K.L.M. Royal Dutch Airlines

3. Sabena

4. Swissair

5. Air France

6. Aer Lingus

7. Alitalia

8. Yugoslav Airlines

PLATE LXXXI FOREIGN AIR LINES

blue, of the British Overseas Airways Corporation and the three Astral Crowns of British European Airways. The proud boast of Scottish Airlines is that their flag, with its stylised Winged Lion, alone displays the Royal Crown. The Red Dragon Flag of Cambrian Air Services was until recent years the emblem of Wales.

Many overseas air lines make an ingenious use of the appropriate national emblem: those of the Commonwealth include the Maple Leaf, Kangaroo and Springbok. The " envelope " design of the Sabena House Flag combines the symbols of Belgium and of the Belgian Congo. The tricolour design of KLM Royal Dutch Airlines is based on the historic *Prinsevlag* of the Netherlands. Pan-American Airways displays a blue globe on a white field (Pls. LXXX, LXXXI).

THE OLYMPIC GAMES

The revival, in modern times, of the athletic contests of Ancient Greece has produced a new emblem, the Olympic Games Flag, which is hoisted, with the national flags of the contestants, over the stadia where the events take place. It displays on a white field an ancient symbol of unity, the chain, consisting of five interlinked circles each of a different colour: blue, yellow, black, green and red (Pl. LXXXII, 1).

THE SALVATION ARMY

The Salvation Army flag is a red rectangle with a broad blue border. In the centre is a yellow star on which the outline of another star is superimposed in red; this contains the words " Blood and Fire " in red (Pl. LXXXII, 2).

THE BOY SCOUTS AND GIRL GUIDES

The Boy Scouts and Girl Guide Associations have
their own flags. The British Boy Scout Flag
displays a fleur-de-lis in gold on a green field;
below this is a scroll bearing the Scout motto " Be
Prepared ". The Girl Guide Flag depicts, in gold
on a blue field, the trefoil which forms the Guide
badge. The threefold nature of the two emblems
symbolises the three promises which the members
of both movements make upon enrolment (Pl.
LXXXII, 3, 4).

THE UNITED NATIONS

Soon after its establishment in 1945, the United
Nations desired a flag to symbolise its ideals. The
first suggestion was to place four vertical bars, long
narrow oblongs, red on a white field, representing
freedom of speech, freedom of worship, freedom
from economic want, and freedom from aggression
(Pl. LXXXIII, 2). It is hardly to be wondered at
that so very uninspiring an emblem should never
have been adopted.

The U.N. preferred for their official emblem,
which also forms their Seal, a map of the world in
Polar Projection with the Greenwich Meridian
vertical: though unavoidably deforming the
southern regions, this nevertheless makes them
recognisable. The map is flanked by two olive-
branches. The United Nations Flag displays the
world symbol in white on a light blue field (Pl.
LXXXIII, 1).

1. Olympic Games

2. Salvation Army

3. Boy Scouts Association (British)

4. Girl Guides Association

PLATE LXXXII. MISCELLANEOUS FLAGS—(i)

THE RED CROSS FLAG AND ITS EQUIVALENTS

In 1863 an International Conference was held at Geneva to consider the mitigation of the hardships of war by care for the sick and wounded. It proposed that all hospitals and kindred services should be regarded as neutral and distinguished by an easily-recognisable flag.

For Christian countries no symbol could be more appropriate than a Cross: the Red Cross Flag accordingly displays a Greek Cross in red on a

1. United Nations

2. Four Freedoms Flag

3. Red Cross

4. Red Crescent

5. Red Lion

PLATE LXXXIII. MISCELLANEOUS FLAGS—(ii)

square white field; this has the further advantage
that it compliments Switzerland, where the
Conference had been held, in forming the Swiss
Flag with its colours reversed (Pl. LXXXIII,3).

As Moslem countries could not be expected to
use a flag bearing a cross, their equivalent emblem
is the Red Crescent Flag, again with a white field
(Pl. LXXXIII, 4). Persia, to whom Cross and
Crescent seem equally unacceptable, has its own
Red Lion Flag, in which the white field bears the
national emblem in red, the lion grasping the sword,
and the sun (Pl. LXXXIII, 5).

INDEX

References in heavy type are to illustrations.

INDEX

INDEX

INDEX

PRINTED BY
LOWE AND BRYDONE (PRINTERS) LTD., LONDON, N.W.10

870. 263